THE
CONSULTING
PROCESS
IN ACTION

Gordon Lippitt
The George Washington University

Ronald Lippitt
Human Resource Development Associates

THE
CONSULTING
PROCESS
IN ACTION

University Associates, Inc.
7596 Eads Avenue
La Jolla, California 92037

Copyright © 1978 by International Authors, B.V.
ISBN: 0-88390-141-2
Library of Congress Catalog Card Number: 77-15681
Printed in the United States of America

To clients, colleagues, students, and family
who have helped us learn consulting
through failures and successes
in the helping process.

Contents

Preface

During the past twenty-five years, we have worked at providing help to persons and groups from all walks of life. One great reward and challenge of people helping is the opportunity to be a learner all the time. The helping process is always a collaborative problem-solving process in which the helper has as much chance to learn as those who are helped.

During the past ten years, our special challenge has been to know how to share with others what we have learned about consulting. Each of us has organized and published some of his learnings, but in this volume, we have shared our learnings with each other. We have organized them in compact form in an effort to contribute to the growing needs of professional and nonprofessional people helpers: consultants, counselors, supervisors, administrators, friends, advisors, and many others.

The most general term for this helping process is consultation. The function of consultation is *part* of the role and function of all those who lead, direct, teach, or interact as friends and peers with others. To simplify our communication, we have addressed all of you as consultants in this volume, although we recognize that consultation may be only one aspect of the job of many of you who also administer, direct, supervise, minister, treat, etc.

At various points, we have distinguished between those help givers who are located in the same setting, organization, or institution as those they are serving. We call these helpers internal consultants, as contrasted to the external consultants who offer their help as outsiders. Often this distinction is important in determining the type of help that is feasible, or appropriate, or credible.

Some of you have had training in consultation as part of your professional school education, others have mostly learned on the job. But,

ix

using our own professional education and experience as a guideline, we are confident that all of us know only a little bit of what there is to learn about being an effective and versatile helper of others. We believe in this volume you will find concepts, strategies, and techniques that will be valuable additions to your repertoire.

In offering you our reflections, experiences, and learnings about consultation, we are mindful of our indebtedness and supports from—

Our graduate students;

The many participants in our workshops on consultation;

Our colleagues, co-consultants, and co-trainers;

Our families, with whom many of the most important confrontations of our concepts and skills have been worked through.

We want particularly to acknowledge our appreciation to Eva Schindler-Rainman, Don Swartz, and Les This, who have collaborated with us for the past ten years in training consultants. In addition, they have reviewed and contributed to portions of this manuscript.

The process of consultation is challenging, awesome, rewarding, and humbling. It is not a science, but as a performing art, it requires the constant growth of those who practice it. We welcome you to some of our growth experiences and learnings.

Gordon Lippitt
Ronald Lippitt

Chapter 1
Consultation: A Need for Competency

Consultation is a two-way interaction—a process of seeking, giving, and receiving help. Consulting is aimed at aiding a person, group, organization, or larger system in mobilizing internal and external resources to deal with problem confrontations and change efforts.

The values, intentions, and behaviors of consultative interaction differ from those of leadership, supervision, evaluation, therapy, and friendship. However, many persons become consultative when carrying out some functions of their primary roles as administrator, supervisor, counselor, therapist, friend, or parent.

The role of a growing number of persons in our society is labeled *consultant* to describe their helping functions. Many of these consultants function as helpers from the outside. Others perform as inside or internal consultants, operating as part of the system they are attempting to help.

HELPERS: PROFESSIONAL AND VOLUNTEER

Throughout history there have been individuals who acquired or were given status and credibility in groups as helpers in solving problems. Tribal wise men, medicine men, and priests often developed special skills as helpers in personal or group problem solving. Although preparation for the helping role did not involve any professional training program, there were apprenticeships and selection for talent. Later, charismatic leaders, such as Buddha, Christ, Muhammad, and Confucius developed circles of followers who, through role modeling, conceptual training, and some supervised practice, developed helping orientations and skills, and presented themselves to people as helpers and change agents.

1

Formal training programs and internships developed as preparation and certification, first for religious ministries and for medical practice, then for psychologists, social workers, and public health workers. Helping tended to be differentiated into consulting and training.

In recent years, individuals have been professionally trained to help solve the problems of all functions of the modern community— business management, labor leadership, education, health, public service, social welfare, recreation, religion, corrections and rehabilitation, personal therapy.

There has also been a resurgence of the amateur or layman helper. The volunteer helper plays a critical role as his "brother's keeper," good neighbor, or citizen volunteer. Perhaps the most exciting development is the general recognition that it is desirable and appropriate to participate in workshops and other programs for learning the skills of helping. An eight-session course, entitled The Helping Person, is a good example of a learning opportunity being widely used by all types of nonprofessionals to develop their helping or consulting skills.

THE GROWING NEED

The most relevant projections of the future emphasize the following trends as important for the future of the consultant role and for the learning of helping skills by persons in all walks of life.

1. One pervasive trend is the rapid rate of technological development with the consequent impact on life styles, social organization of enterprises, and the political and economic systems of the community, state, and nation. Increasingly complex problems of interdependence, welfare, education, leadership, and decision making are being created. There is a much greater need for persons and groups to collaborate, to ask for and to give help and support to each other. But the motivations and skills of people lag far behind the increased need and the increased knowledge of how to solve problems, how to generate and use resources, and how to set up collaborative efforts.

2. A related trend is that more and more people have discretionary time to spend beyond the demands of wage-earning time and life-maintenance activities. This time is available for creative, developmental volunteer activities. The quality of community life and the quality of individual lives could be improved if interpersonal helping and support becomes a valued and skilled activity. "Good neighboring" could become a rewarding priority and a revitalization of democracy.

3. A third trend, which should grow in strength, is the awareness that there is a crisis with human energy, as well as with physical energy. At the core of the human energy issue are the cumulating analyses and growing awareness of the under-utilization, underdevelopment, and misuse of human resources—neglected racial and ethnic minority groups, women, children and youth, the handicapped, the elderly, the unemployed, the undereducated. This is a great challenge to both professional and volunteer helpers.

4. A consequence of these three trends, which is a trend itself, is the fact that the needs for help are accelerating faster than the preparation of professional helpers—consultants, trainers, teachers. This means the need for volunteers and paraprofessional aides will continue to increase very rapidly. Top priority should be given to the recruiting and training of volunteers and aides in the skills of helping and supporting and to the creating of teams of professionals and volunteers as helping-consulting teams.

UTILIZATION OF RESOURCES

A large proportion of the personnel connected with knowledge re-source centers have little interest in the role of helper. They focus on the production of knowledge or the conceptual integration of such knowledge, rather than on its utilization in arenas of action. Others who are interested in giving help remain so specialized in an area of knowl-edge that they can be helpful in only a small number of situations and over a narrow spectrum of problems. Often, they are oriented toward functioning alone as consultants, rather than working in teams that could offer complementary resources to the practical problem solvers. In general, those who have a disciplined knowledge base or an inte-grated conceptual perspective have received no training in the skills of helping or in the training and supervising of volunteers. They have little ability to identify with the situations of potential clients, and tend to be quite impatient and directive in their interaction styles.

Unfortunately, the territorial attitudes of university departments, the specializations of disciplines, and the lack of curriculum collabora-tion between the departments and the professional schools greatly inhibits the development of well-oriented, appropriately motivated and skilled, problem-solving consultants and leaders of helping teams.

By their orientation, those who need help also contribute to the lack of effective utilization of consultation. A typical crisis orientation means that, usually, serious pain must be felt before there is motivation to seek help, and then the time pressures for solution make effective consultation very difficult.

Another serious and pervasive block is the evaluation that to "do it yourself" is the greatest sign of competence and asking for help is a symptom of weakness. Because the highest value is placed on the line people who are the producers, there is reluctance to invest in staff people, such as internal consultants. If help is needed, there is a tendency to depend on inside resources in order to "keep it in the family." Often, the specific type of help needed to work on particular problems is not available within the organization, but people are reluctant or lack sophistication on how to seek the appropriate outside help.

To summarize, the potential users of consultants are uninformed about identifying, recruiting, and utilizing consultation resources. They tend to reject diagnosis as a necessary starting point for working toward the solution of a particular problem. They lack perspective on necessary budget requirements; and they are not oriented toward using methodological help in problem solving, instead of "having somebody give us the answers."

This is only a small sample of the reasons why the use of consultation resources lags so far behind the need and why the professionals and volunteers who are attempting to fill consultant roles are relatively unprepared to do flexible, competent jobs in different problem-solving situations.

DIMENSIONS OF THE HELPING PROCESS

The following are some of the dimensions we use in thinking about giving effective help in any consultation situation. Later chapters will fill in this framework.

Phases of Consultation

It is useful to think of the consultation process in terms of six phases. These phases and the types of helping work that both the client and the consultant must do in each phase are examined in Chapter Two.

Consultation Roles or Functions

The functional differences and similarities between internal and external consultants, and between professional and volunteer helpers, are delineated in Chapter Three, along with the ways in which these differences of position and responsibility affect the kind of help each can give. A dozen different role functions are identified, so that a consultant can clarify his or her role and function at any point in the process of giving help. Every competent helper must be flexible enough to function in a variety of roles.

Types of Client Systems

In some cases, the client system is a person or a small interpersonal unit, such as a couple or a family; in others, the client may be a small group (e.g., a team, a committee, a staff unit). The client may be a total organizational system (e.g., a company, agency, bureau, association); or it may be an interorganizational system, such as a community, a state or nation, or an international system. The size of the client system influences decisions concerning the credibility and competencies required of the consultant and the type and size of consultation design.

Some consultants tend to specialize and work with certain types of client systems. Other consultants are generalists with respect to types of client systems, but specialize in terms of the kinds of problems they help with and the methods they use.

Clients can be classified according to their type of functions, operations, and products, for example:

- Economic systems: business, industry, chambers of commerce, associations;
- Political systems: political parties, city governments, League of Women Voters, governor's offices;
- Educational systems: schools, colleges, adult education programs, state departments of education;
- Religious systems: churches, seminaries, monasteries;
- Recreational and leisure-time systems: recreation programs, agencies, parks, camps, hobby clubs;
- Cultural enrichment systems: theaters, museums, art schools, musical societies;
- Welfare systems: poverty programs, unemployment programs, food programs, subsidized housing;
- Health systems: hospitals, clinics, health education;
- Social protection agencies: courts, police, legal aid, civil liberties;
- Mass communication systems: newspapers, radio, television;
- Geographic entities: neighborhoods, communities, counties, regions.

Currently, all these systems have programs for recruiting, training, and using professional and volunteer helpers, but the needs are greater than the resources. The opportunities for professional consultants and trained volunteer helpers are growing in all these parts of community and national life.

Contracts and Focuses

A helping relationship may vary greatly in duration and sequence; for example, it may be:

- A one-contact relationship, a single consultation, a one-day institute, or a brief workshop;
- A single major contact with a sequence of follow-up supportive relationships;
- A defined series of sessions, e.g., six weekly sessions, a semester course, a three-phase training program;
- An indeterminant helping contract, with termination to be mutually determined when the work is done.

It may be informally defined, or a formal consulting contract may be developed.

The consultant must appropriately focus his or her helping efforts to promote the problem-solving work that is needed. Sometimes, the focus is on:

- The functioning of a total system, e.g., the whole family, the staff group, the total agency;
- A subpart of the client system, e.g., the mother, the company president, one department;
- One function or problem of the client, e.g., goal setting, removing stereotypes, improving trust, making decisions more efficiently;
- The relationship between two persons, two or more groups, or inter-agency relationships.

A helping intervention can also be focused in terms of the type of work to be done. For example, the efforts of the consultant may be focused on certain kinds of task work or process work. Task work may include mobilizing resources, setting goals, clarifying values, projecting alternatives, developing evaluation plans, and the many other focuses mentioned in Chapter Two. Process work may focus on mediating conflicts, developing trust, uncovering hidden agendas, and identifying blockages in communication.

DEVELOPING CONSULTATION SKILLS

This introductory chapter has emphasized and clarified the increasing importance in our local and national life of the process of asking for and giving help. There is a wide range of problem-solving and change confrontations in which complex issues of interdependence, decision making, and action require great skill and understanding from helpers.

Whether these helpers are volunteer neighbors or professional consultants, they need training in the values, attitudes, and skills of giving help—of providing effective consultation. Professional helpers have a growing responsibility to train volunteers and to build helping teams that include persons with appropriate formal training for the consultant role.

In this volume, we provide some basic orientations to helping, some designs and tools for skill development, and some examples of "how to do it" from our experience and training.

Chapter 2
Phases in Consulting

Each step in the process of consulting confronts the helper and the client with a series of interaction decisions and possible alternatives for behavioral strategy. These interaction decisions and behaviors primarily may be the responses of a would-be helper to the expressions of need, concern, or pain of a client (person or group), or they may be initiated by the helper to stimulate a desire for help, to establish a helping contract, and to activate problem-solving efforts on the part of the client.

These interactions may be part of the informal process of give-and-take between peers—a voluntary context of friendship; a more deliberative effort of a parent, an older friend, or a more experienced person to give help on a problem; or the efforts of a professional helper—doctor, lawyer, social worker, psychologist, organization development (OD) specialist, etc.—to formally provide contracted helping services. The helper may be inside the same group or system as the client (e.g. an internal consultant, member of the same family, or supervisor in the same department) or may be an external helper, offering the more removed perspective of an outsider.

According to our experience, the phases of the consulting process are equally applicable to all types of helping relationships and positions, but there are some significant differences in roles and intervention decisions during consultation activities.

The steps or focuses we have identified in a consultant-client working relationship fall into six major phases:

1. Initial contact or entry;
2. Formulating a contract and establishing a helping relationship;
3. Problem identification and diagnostic analysis;
4. Setting goals and planning for action;

8

5. Taking action and cycling feedback;

6. Contract completion: continuity, support, and termination.

The following is a brief review of the types of working tasks (work focuses) that seem to be involved in each of these phases. Included as part of the discussion of each work focus are excerpts from a series of taped dialogues by the authors as we shared illustrative case situations from our consulting experiences.

PHASE I. CONTACT AND ENTRY

Work Focus 1. Making First Contact

The initial exploration of a potential consulting relationship may come from the following three sources.

The potential client. A sense of pain or a problem may be interpreted as a need to seek help, accompanied by an awareness that certain kinds of consultation may be an appropriate source of help. Or there may be no pain, but instead a desire to increase one's competitive advantage by improving productivity and effectiveness or to improve satisfaction with one's self-image. It may be the normal operating procedure of the organization to seek out and use consultants. Contacting a particular consultant or consulting group may be a result of previous experience, awareness of the consultant's reputation, knowledge of the consultant's specialization in particular problems, or merely a shopping expedition to find out what is available.

The potential consultant. Contact may be motivated by a general search for new clients or the consultant's knowledge that he or she has been helpful to another similar client system. The consultant may perceive a pattern of functional ineffectiveness similar to that which he or she has coped with before. The consultant may have particular priorities, such as helping any group trying to improve the quality of the environment or developing student participation in decision making.

A third party. Someone who perceives a need for help in a client system may be aware of the skills and resources available through consultation. This third party undertakes to bring the client and the consultant together. The initiative may be no more than a referral suggestion or as much as a formal three-way meeting. The third party who is a power figure in the client system may simply retain the consultant and assign him or her to help where it seems to be needed. Such an executive may perceive that "they need to be upgraded" or "they need a shot in the arm" and make the decision that a consultant will best serve such a purpose.

Whether the potential consultant is an insider or an outsider makes some differences in this contact initiation. Typically, the insider knows more about the existence of difficulties or pain. On the other hand, it is probably harder for the potential client to admit a need for help to a peer within the system. Referral by a third party is probably easier for the insider because it is more convenient, more legitimate, and less expensive.

The outsider generally has a more difficult time than the insider in taking the initiative because of the problem of credible entry from the outside. Conversely, the outsider probably has some advantage because a client system often finds it easier to share a problem with an outsider. The client system may also assume greater expertness on the part of the outsiders as compared to the more familiar faces inside the system. Referral by a third party establishes a link between an outsider and a system.

EXAMPLES FROM OUR EXPERIENCES

Ron: A frequent type of initiative by a potential client is a telephone call. Fairly typical is a recent call from a professional school, asking if I would be interested in doing some kind of a program in professional and personal development and growth with doctoral candidates in a field internship program. After probing a bit to find out what they wanted, I decided they needed to think it through a little more before I could clearly respond whether I would be an appropriate resource. I asked a number of questions and suggested that they write answers to the questions in a letter within the next day or two. I promised either to respond with a memo on what I might be able to do to meet their needs (as I understood them) or to make a referral to some other, more appropriate, resource.

They wrote a good letter and my response was a four-page, rather carefully developed memorandum, offering two alternative ideas about desirable outcomes and types of designs for helping. I included information on different levels of budget for the two alternatives and some of the initial data collection I would be asking them to do.

Gordon: Yes, telephone calls are a very frequent first approach. I had a funny call the other day. A personnel director from a large pharmaceutical firm wanted me to meet with him and some others. When I asked the purpose of the meeting, he said, "Well, we need to have you talk with us about some OD work." When I asked about the kind of OD work, he said, "We'd just like to have you come and talk with us, and we'll pay a stipend for exploration." I discovered that the president of the firm was interested in assessing me, so we arranged to have lunch together.

Although the president of the firm was very affable and asked me some questions that weren't necessarily related to the project, the luncheon was definitely a testing of our mutual chemistry and my competency. The firm's OD director and the personnel director were there, ready to implement any further planning if the testing worked out. They called the next day with an O.K. to go ahead and do some exploratory planning.

Ron: Don't you think it is important when responding to these first contact initiatives to be very open in probing and sharing where you are?

Gordon: Yes, I think that's crucial. I recently received a letter from a community college that had issues concerning minority groups and faculty decision making. The college people wanted a problem-solving session of two days. I answered that letter very honestly and critically, explaining the impossibility of their expectations. I presented an alternative pattern with the probable conditions of contract and cost, but indicated that I didn't expect they would want to go ahead because this was going to be quite different from their objectives.

Surprisingly, they called back saying they were so impressed by my openness in confronting the unreality of their expectations that they wanted to go ahead with us rather than take one of the other bids that had accepted their assumptions. How about an example in which you have taken the initiative to try to get a client involved?

Ron: In one example, which was successful, we wrote two invitation letters, about a week apart, to a sample of potential clients—in this case, small businesses in the area.

The first letter was a warm-up, explaining who we were and some of our experiences with businesses similar to their own—in terms of new organization development procedures that were proving helpful in economic survival.

The second letter was a specific invitation to attend a three-hour luncheon session. At the luncheon, we provided a sample micro-event with some input by us and some active participation by the guests, using models of goal setting and brainstorming, and identifying some of the major kinds of dilemmas that required their problem-solving efforts. The event ended with an opportunity for the guests to become involved in a consultative project, really a three-phase process of fact finding and consultation. We provided a handout on this process for them to take along and think about and we promised to make a follow-up telephone call to see whether they would like to explore the opportunity.

Typically, out of fifteen to twenty invitations we would get eight to ten participants at the luncheon and two to four follow-up relationships that developed into client contracts.

Gordon: Very frequently, one of our successful initiatives begins with participants we meet in a training activity who chat with us individually about their own situations. We suggest a follow-up contact to become acquainted with their situation and to explore the possibilities for following through on ideas they have acquired in the training activity. What kind of third-party entry situations come to your mind?

Ron: One of the most frequent problems in my experience is how to turn a coercive situation into a voluntary participation and learning activity. For example, there was the school administrator who asked us to work with his staff on ways to implement new accountability legislation that required the adoption and development of annual personnel review and assessment procedures. The challenge was how to convert this relatively negative entry situation into a collaboration in which the participants could become actively involved, see the payoff value to themselves, and learn that the consultant is not a tool of the administrator.

Gordon: Yes, in a recent situation, I had to work out a relationship difference between a state director, who was employing me, and the planning committee of the state staff, which was representing the client system. I began by being a third party, bringing the other two parties together to clarify some joint goals. Sometimes an entry situation is even more difficult when the president of the company assigns an internal consultant to "fix up that unproductive department."

Work Focus 2. Helping Identify and Clarify the Need for Change

After making contact, tentative entry into a working relationship includes some important processes of exploration. This second work focus involves the consultant in either helping the potential client to explain his understanding of the problem or obtaining information about activities within parts of the system that might help isolate and identify the problem.

Sometimes the potential consultant functions as a legitimatized listener and asker of questions; sometimes he/she is an inquiry expert with tools for conducting an assessment of needs. Sometimes a potential helper must cope with a lack of sensitivity to the need for change or with a lack of a sense of responsibility or with an inability to enter into or put energy into any kind of change effort. These problems may require the consultant to call the attention of the potential client to the ways in which other systems have identified and worked on similar problems. Often, there is a need for group interviewing in which persons occupying different positions in the system stimulate each other's articulation of perceptions of relevant issues and problems. Such openness can be legitimatized by the objectivity of the interview situation and by the questions asked by the consultant-interviewer.

If we consider consulting advantages and disadvantages, the insider usually is better prepared to probe, listen, and clarify, but probing is likely to create defensiveness because of his/her in-the-family status. The outsider has the disadvantage of lacking the context and history of the particular system and its operational problems.

EXAMPLES FROM OUR EXPERIENCES

Ron: The group interview is one of the most valuable ways to help potential clients identify and clarify their needs. For a recent community project, in which an interagency council wanted to explore problems of poor communication and cooperation, we conducted a series of five group interviews. There were six or seven people in each group, and each group was heterogeneous, with the members coming from different agencies. In these interviews, the participants stimulated each other, and their interactions gave us a great deal of data about the issues of communication and collaboration.

Gordon: I often use a quick, anonymous, written survey with key management people. Then I get them together for a feedback session in which we share my data, probe their interpretations, and amplify what has been revealed in the survey statements.

Ron: Another helpful technique is asking a small representative group to simulate being an outside committee making an assessment of its organization. During the simulated visit, the observers describe what they see that pleases them as some of the strengths of the organization, and what they are sorry to see and wish could be changed in order for the organization to function more effectively. This kind of listing, based on brainstorming from a perspective of outside objectivity, is very helpful in getting out the data.

Work Focus 3. Exploring the Readiness for Change

This is important, mutually shared work in which the consultant explores the readiness of the client system to devote time, energy, and the committed involvement of appropriate people to a problem-solving process. The client system, on the other hand, explores the capability, sensitivity, credibility, and trustworthiness of the potential consultant.

Usually, the outside consultant is able openly to test the readiness of the potential client. The inside consultant, whose qualifications are already known to the client system, should be sensitive to the potential impediments to involvement and collaboration for change that might occur during the working relationship.

Work Focus 4. Exploring the Potential for Working Together

Here, each of the parties explores and tests the potentialities for an effective working relationship. Familiarity can lead the client system to stereotyped preconceptions of the inside consultant's particular responses, which may be quite incorrect. The potential client may have conscious or unconscious fears about the difficulties of withdrawing from a working relationship with the inside consultant, as contrasted to the greater ease of terminating a contract with an outsider. The outsider frequently is able more readily to clarify the nature of available resources. Many outside consultants consider it important to propose a period of testing for compatibility before making mutual commitments for a long-term working relationship.

EXAMPLES FROM OUR EXPERIENCES

Ron: To explore readiness for change, we have found it helpful with several clients to develop, with their help, a list of good reasons for not having time or motivation or inclination to get involved in a change effort, and a parallel list of reasons for becoming involved. We make this into a check sheet, asking clients to check the items on both sides that are true of themselves, to give some value weighting to the most important ones on each side, and then to use the list as a basis for discussing where they are. This kind of procedure legitimatizes any hidden agendas of resistance and gets things out in the open for sharing and decision making.

Gordon: Frequently, I ask the person who is negotiating with me to identify all the key people who would be involved in collaborating with my consultation and to convene them in an ad hoc session. This allows me to have an open discussion with these people about who I am and why I've been invited in, and it encourages them to ask any clarifying questions, make any statements of doubt or support, etc.

Ron: I had quite a time recently in a large hospital. I was exploring and probing to discover who the client system really would be. It was a chance to meet with the different clusters of personnel, giving them a chance to examine me, what kind of control they would have over the process of working, and what my expectations would be if we worked together. I had to meet with about six such clusters before going back to the administrator to clarify and define potential working relationships.

Gordon: I frequently try a kind of microcosm of what working together would be like. Usually, I involve people in some activities, some brainstorming, and a little bit of process observation, and I offer some input about typical activities done in an organization development program such as they are considering. This helps to surface differences in orientation, readiness, and commitment.

PHASE II.   FORMULATING A CONTRACT AND ESTABLISHING A HELPING RELATIONSHIP

The four work focuses of Phase I should produce at least a tentative decision on the part of both consultant and client either to discontinue the exploration or to move toward some kind of agreement about the nature, objectives, and conditions of a working relationship. We have identified three focuses of work in the second phase.

Work Focus 5. What Outcomes Are Desired?

It is not enough just to agree that there is a problem or that a change is desirable. In clarifying a potential working relationship, it is important to explore what kinds of outcomes might be achieved—or would be desirable—if the working relationship is successful. Would the goal be an increase in profits? A change in the public image of the system? A change in the motivation of the workers or in the working relationship between supervisors and their subordinates? This certainly will not be the final statement of objectives, but it should provide a basis for the mutual understanding needed to formulate a contract.

In this type of work, the inside consultant has a better grasp of feasibility and need, but may have too much of a negative problem orientation. The outside consultant may be better able to invoke a wider perspective on possible goals and a more brainstorming approach toward desirable outcomes.

EXAMPLES FROM OUR EXPERIENCES

Gordon: With more and more clients, I'm finding it worthwhile to spend quite a bit of initial time trying to get concrete about what changes they would like in the way they are operating. Although goal setting typically comes later in a consulting relationship, it is important to probe clients for the concrete outcomes they want from any kind of developmental or change effort, which usually means stretching their thinking.

Ron: I certainly agree with you. Recently, I met with representatives of a large church to explore whether we might work together.

I asked them to play the roles that leaders of the church would have five years hence and to make a list of things that pleased them concerning the progress made in those five years. They became very involved in this listing and began to clarify and considerably change their ideas about what they were after.

Work Focus 6. Who Should Do What?

The client has a strong need to know how much time and energy and commitment the consultant is ready to put into a helping relationship. And the consultant has a strong need for clarification about who should be involved, what kinds of activity would be feasible, what kind of support could be expected from the top power structure, what kind of financial and time commitments would be made, and how the contract would be terminated. At this stage, it is crucial to determine who the client system really is, particularly to discover whether there is a difference between the client system and the individual or office that pays the bills.

Work Focus 7. Time Perspective and Accountability

Another part of formulating the contract includes clarifying the projected time period allowed for accomplishing the desired outcomes and the evaluation procedures to be used in assessing progress toward the desired outcomes. This time perspective may include agreement about milestones at which the progress of the working relationship will be reviewed and decisions about continuation or termination will be made.

Because of an ongoing structural relationship to the client system, the inside consultant probably has a more difficult time arriving at some criteria for evaluation and termination or continuation. However, the inside consultant certainly should be closer to the flow of data about the success or nonsuccess of the helping efforts. The outside consultant may have an easier time proposing objective evaluation procedures and obtaining the client's commitment to provide the necessary data for evaluation. But the outside consultant usually works with the time perspective of a much more ad hoc relationship, with accountability being expected much sooner.

EXAMPLES FROM OUR EXPERIENCES

Gordon: I'm finding that more and more clients are ready to develop written agreements. Frequently, there is a discussion with certain members of the client system about who will do what, and the timing, etc., but the contract about financial arrangements is with somebody else in a different office. This can bring about some real problems. For example, recently we had worked out the arrangements for a three-day workshop for the top executives of a national government agency. But then the agency postponed the event because the contract office had some questions that hadn't been answered and some forms that had to be signed.

Ron: For things such as time schedule and commitments, we have found it helpful to develop a first draft of the contract and then to say, in essence, "I need to check this out with colleagues who are going to be involved, and I would like you to do the same. Because both parties tend to forget some things that become very important later, we need to have a critical review before finalizing anything."

Frequently, the persons who are negotiating the working relationship become so enthusiastic about doing the project that they neglect certain expense items or become unrealistic about time schedule, or give low priority to some things that are very important to other people.

Gordon: Another important aspect of contracting is having a tryout or a pilot project of limited duration and magnitude, before asking either party to go into something larger and long term. For example, in a recent team-building program with a large school system, we asked for a small pilot project within two buildings, with careful observation and documentation by some internal staff members in order to assess and review the feasibility of the design and the results that might be expected. This relieved a lot of pressure, provided some good testing on feasibility, and was a good basis for developing a working relationship; it made a larger, more comprehensive design workable and fundable.

PHASE III. PROBLEM IDENTIFICATION AND DIAGNOSTIC ANALYSIS

Processes of entry and contract formulation involve preliminary diagnostic activity, readiness for change, and the dynamics of a working relationship. This is all preliminary to the much more intensive diagnostic work and planning for action required in any successful consultative relationship.

Work Focus 8. Force-Field Diagnosis

Force-field diagnosis is a model or method for identifying the forces that impede movement toward current goals and the forces that facilitate such movement. The client system is likely to encounter problems in providing opportunities for the data collection and staff involvement that are requested by the consultant, and the consultant is responsible for being focused and sensitive in fact-finding efforts. Confronting the consultant is the responsibility of helping the client to interpret the causes of problems and the implications for change.

The inside consultant, usually aware of the existence of diagnostic data, is able to recommend appropriate targets for data collection, but being "in the family" is more likely to create defensiveness and resistance. Normally, it is easier for the external consultant to request and require unfamiliar types of data collection and to use new methodologies and tools.

EXAMPLES FROM OUR EXPERIENCE

Gordon: The force-field diagram, shown in Figure 1, is an important tool in helping clients gain perspective on the numerous blocks and inhibitions, supports and resources, in their operations. Recently, when working with the staff of a government agency, I put two sheets of newsprint on the wall and diagramed the force-field. From the brainstorming of the group members, I was able to list on one sheet the supports and resources they had for accomplishing their work goal. On the other sheet, they identified the restraints and blocks they experienced in trying to get things done. In each case, they indicated whether the support or the block came from inside of themselves, from certain norms and traditions of the group, or from traditions and characteristics of their environment, such as the budget, regulations, and physical setting. Then they prioritized the resources they were inadequately utilizing and the blocks they should eliminate.

Ron: A different use for the force-field, applicable in the phase-four examination of planning, is to write a projected goal at the top of the force-field diagram and identify the potential resources and restraints for moving toward the goal. This provides much data for planning.

Gordon: There's still a third use of the force-field: during phase five, when some action strategy has been selected and the task is one of mobilizing for action. In this case, I write the action steps at the top of the force-field diagram. We look at the resources and supports for taking the action and the kinds of traps we should be sensitive to in order to insure success. All three uses of the force-field diagnostic procedure are helpful tools in consultation and should be clearly differentiated from each other.

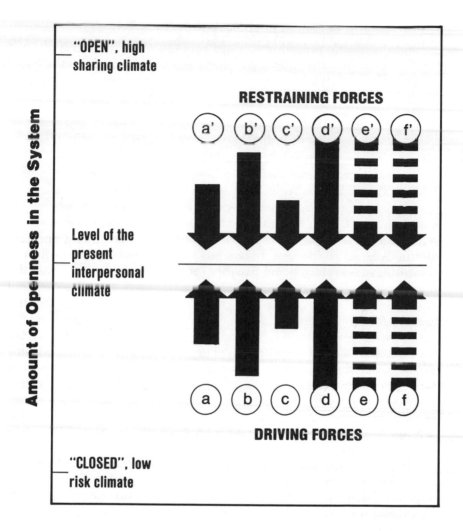

Figure 1. The force-field analysis model
(Adapted from M. S. Spier, "Kurt Lewin's 'Force Field Analysis,'" in J. E. Jones & J. W. Pfeiffer (Eds.), *The 1973 Annual Handbook for Group Facilitators*. La Jolla, Calif.: University Associates, 1973. Reprinted by permission of the publisher.)

PHASE IV. GOAL SETTING AND PLANNING

A good diagnostic procedure should provide the basic warmup for a productive goal-setting process. This process must include the complementary activity of step-by-step planning of the work required to reach a goal.

Work Focus 9. Projecting Goals

Having acquired a diagnostic sensitivity to "where we are" and "what our operating problems are," the client is ready for the challenge of looking ahead. Typically, looking ahead is aided by surveys of what is wanted and needed by those we serve, the pains and problems we are experiencing, the predictions of what things are going to be like, and our own values—what we would most like to see develop from possible alternatives for the future. To set meaningful goals we must have a clear idea of a preferred and feasible future. This provides a basis for planning.

EXAMPLES FROM OUR EXPERIENCE

Ron: An interesting illustration of projecting long-range goals is that of a large national organization. The organization's planning committee started with current goals and a survey of goal priorities and projected eight areas from which goals needed to be developed. The committee commissioned a team to review the data on trends and the projections written by groups of futurists, and then, from their analyses, to project three or four alternative and possible futures. These alternative-future statements became the basis for goal-setting workshops throughout the organization, in which leaders identified their preferred future and explained the rationale for their choice and the efforts needed to create that particular future.

Gordon: Often, I find it helpful to begin by providing a client with input on some major trends in the society—economic, political, social, etc. I did this recently with a state health department, and the staff members were stimulated to look at the relevance of societal trends for their own departmental future. The staff members projected specific images of their operation five years hence, taking into account the trends of which they had become aware, the developmental trends in their own organization, and their vision of a future optimized with their own evaluations of good practices.

**Work Focus 10. Planning for Action and Involvement:
What, Who, and How?**

When planning the implementation of meaningful goals the key is a sequence of steps toward a goal, often simultaneous steps by different persons or groups. Criteria—evidences—of when a step has been achieved must be identified, so that there can be clear indications that the group is on the right path or needs to change direction and to provide a basis for celebration, which is the basis for continuing motivation and group spirit.

One of the most critical and neglected phases of planning is an *anticipatory rehearsal*. It helps to answer the question of who (from inside or from outside the system) should be involved in order for a plan of action to have the best probability of success. Once these targets for involvement in planning are identified, a second question becomes how to involve them. This sets up new planning sequences and new goals that are concentrated on involvement strategy.

The inside consultant probably has more knowledge and more access to knowledge about the potential resource value of persons and units who should be involved at various stages in the problem-solving action. However, it is also more difficult for the inside consultant to request the participation of high power figures in the client system and the involvement of parts of the system that are uncommitted but crucial. The outside consultant often has great leverage with respect to involvement.

PHASE V. TAKING ACTION AND CYCLING FEEDBACK

The payoff is in the successful taking of action and in the continuity of the long-term gains after the first bursts of energy and effort are expended. We have identified three work focuses of the critical implementation phase.

Work Focus 11. Successful Taking of Action

In the fifth phase of consulting, a key function of the consultant is the skill development necessary for increasing the probability that the action taken will be successful rather than abortive. Another element is supporting celebrations of small successes on a step-by-step path of action. *The major motivation for continuing effort comes from frequent experiences of successful movement on a defined path that leads somewhere*. The successful consultant also works with key parts of the client system to coordinate multiple activities and the involvement of individuals and units.

The inside consultant enjoys more continuous observation of activity and a better assessment of levels of skill and needs for skill development. The outside consultant probably has greater leverage for introducing skill-development activities and for initiating stop sessions in which to look at progress and to review process issues in order to ensure optimal focus of energy on work and support relationships.

EXAMPLES FROM OUR EXPERIENCES

Ron: The opportunity and responsibility for helping the client celebrate has become increasingly important to me. A recent example is my work with a group of thirteen compensatory education teams, made up of teachers, aides, and volunteers from center-city schools.

The members of each team projected some goals of what they would like to have happen in the classroom and in their own performances within six months. They developed a series of criteria of progress toward their goals, and through brainstorming they decided to stop at least every two or three weeks to check on evidence of progress. They identified fourteen different ways in which they might have meaningful celebrations, ranging all the way from going to the principal to explain how well they were getting along, to food celebrations with their classrooms, to having a drink together after school.

It has been exciting to hear about their various celebrations and the ways in which these events have provided a continuing basis for group cohesion and motivation.

Gordon: I think the whole notion of anticipatory preparation for action tends to be neglected. Rehearsal or simulation is very important, and I try to help most of my client systems to work on anticipatory preparation.

A departmental group I was working with in a large company arrived at the point of needing involvement, support, and sanction from top management. After briefing me in the role of top manager, they practiced their presentation, using feedback from me and from each other for improving their skills of presentation. They made a lot of improvements and felt good when they were successful.

Ron: Various kinds of process interventions can help groups to improve their action by stopping and looking at how they are doing and how they might be improving their action. We made very active use of stop sessions while working with the ward teams of a large psychiatric facility on improving their clinical decision making and planning in regard to individual patients. After the teams had been working for fifteen or twenty minutes on a particular case conference, we would intervene for a minute to have them each check a little stop-session sheet, rating their feelings of how well they were being listened to, how well they were listening to others, and how they were doing in decision making. They shared their data, becoming consultants for themselves with ideas for improving their operating procedure, and within five to eight minutes moved ahead to continue their work, typically with many evidences of improvement.

Gordon: Another helpful procedure is having a little internal reality-testing team listen to planning or decision-making sessions with the responsibility of intervening to raise questions about feasibility, omissions, or people who should be involved but are not being considered, etc. This reality testing can be a rotating function of pairs or trios within the group.

Work Focus 12. Evaluation and Guiding Feedback

Using appropriate procedures to elicit feedback about progress and to involve the necessary persons in the assessment of this feedback is a crucial part of the consultant's role during the action phase. This continuing assessment of the consequences of action can save more dollars, hours, and energy than any other of the consultant's helping efforts.

With the advantage of being in closer touch with the change process, the internal consultant usually is more able to secure feedback at strategic points, but there also may be greater motivation to hide problems from him or her. The outside consultant can more easily introduce new methodologies for getting feedback data and can legitimately convene analysis and feedback sessions with appropriate personnel.

Work Focus 13. Revising Action and Mobilizing Additional Resources

Feedback is only helpful if it is utilized rapidly to re-examine goals, to revise action strategies, and, perhaps, to activate decisions concerning the mobilization of additional resources and changes of assignments and roles.

The inside consultant may be in a better position to be aware of needed but unused resources, at least those within the system. But the outside consultant has an advantage in utilizing the data to confront blockages and resistances to effective action and probably offers better perspective in suggesting alternative courses of action and the need for external resources.

EXAMPLES FROM OUR EXPERIENCES

Ron: Collecting evaluation data is really a waste of time unless some planning and energy are put into processing and using the findings, rewarding those who have made relevant efforts, and revising and improving plans for the next stages of action.

I had an interesting client situation with a school system and a PTA. I had been helping them to collaborate on developing a procedure for the sharing of decision making, goal setting, and action planning by school administrators, board members, teachers, parents, and students. The evaluation procedure involved group interviews with each of the subpopulations conducted by trained pairs of teachers, students, parents, or administrators. The data focused on feelings about the problems, the successes, and the issues that had been experienced. The important feature was the feedback teams, consisting of a parent, teacher, student, and administrator. In a series of sessions, table groups of five to seven listened to the findings, presented one or two at a time by the feedback teams. The groups brainstormed implications for improvement of communication and collaboration, reported these, and at each session arrived at some priorities for next steps and some conclusions about the values and strengths of what they had been doing.

Gordon: It's desirable to think about a consultant getting feedback about how people are reacting to him or her, as well as stimulating feedback within the client system. After a day or two with clients, I give them a little check sheet to record their reactions to my efforts and to suggest ways in which I might be more helpful. The clients seem to like this, and it certainly gives me some helpful data for revising my efforts.

Ron: An evaluation issue that comes up fairly frequently is the pressure to cut funds that presumably were allocated in the budget for documentation and evaluation. This has made me more sensitive about getting a clear statement about evaluation into the consultation contract and keeping it before the client as a continuing value and responsibility. Of course, one key thing is to demonstrate how helpful evaluation can be.

Gordon: I believe documentation is one of the most neglected aspects of the work of consultants with clients. Without good documentation of what has gone on, it is difficult to pass on to internal consultants many of the designs and activities that have worked well and should be continued. It is also very difficult to report to policy boards and to outside funding sources what has been done and how helpful it has been. And, finally, most organizations that have a successful development program or develop innovations in their ways of operating should be responsible enough to share these learnings with other agencies needing this type of resource.

PHASE VI. CONTRACT COMPLETION: CONTINUITY, SUPPORT, TERMINATION

The greatest problem with much change and consultation effort is that the changes achieved are short-run and are followed by regression to old patterns; or are only a fragile, poor continuity of the new status; or are marked by the growth of counter-reactions that should be coped with quickly in order to guarantee the continuity of the change. Much consultation design does not include a plan for follow-up support or provisions for gradual termination of the consultant's help and installation within the system of the successfully used resources.

Work Focus 14. Designing for Continuity Supports

The designing of support systems for the successful continuity of change efforts is perhaps the most significant test of the competence and professional quality of the consultant. Sometimes this is a plan for a continuing review of events, including and involving a wide circle of personnel from the client system. Often there is a program of support conference calls with the consultant to check on deadlines. Another type of support design involves the documentation, write-up, and reporting through publication and professional meetings of successful innovations.

The inside consultant is present on a continuing basis to observe where and when additional support is needed to maintain the new structures, roles, or processes. The outside consultant is in a strong position to negotiate periodic reviews and to provide skill training for the involvement of new personnel or inside change agents.

Work Focus 15. Termination Plans

A professional responsibility and goal of most consultants is to become progressively unnecessary. Consultants design for this in various ways, including:

- Training an insider to take over the functions initiated by the outsider;
- Setting a series of dates for decreased budget and involvement of outside helpers;
- Having a termination celebration for the final product of a collaborative effort, e.g., a publication;
- Establishing a minimal periodic maintenance plan, such as an annual review session.

The key notion is that every consultation relationship must have some plan for a healthy, mutually satisfying termination of the working relationship. Established early in the working relationship, this fact helps guide many intervention decisions during all phases of consultation.

EXAMPLES FROM OUR EXPERIENCES

Ron: I have found the development of temporary task forces most helpful in organization development continuities. Each has a convener, an agenda, and a time sequence of meetings. Usually before discontinuing my active relationship, I sit in on at least the first session and work with the internal coordinator on plans for receiving reports and reconvening the groups. In one such situation, each group had a consultation period with me to present its plans for work, for a time schedule, and for the product the group would produce by a deadline that was determined by the group itself but committed publicly.

Gordon: One important continuity procedure is to develop a close working relationship with one or more persons inside the system who have been designated as having the continuing role of internal consultant or change agent. I work extensively with them during my time with the client system, and later I am available to them by telephone, or I make a periodic visitation on their request to help support the work.

Ron: The potentialities of periodic telephone consultations are not appreciated or utilized enough by most consultants. Currently, in one situation where I have been working with teams in several branches of the same agency, each team has a little telephone amplifier box. On a monthly basis, we have a conference call with each team sitting around its amplifier box, allowing us to have discussions of progress, successes, and ideas for next steps.

FINAL COMMENT

We have found this framework of phases and work focuses useful in our own consulting practice and in helping many internal consultants and outside helpers to clarify their roles and guide their intervention decisions. In the next two chapters, we examine in more detail the multiple roles of consultation and the challenges and dilemmas encountered in making appropriate intervention decisions.

Chapter 3
Multiple Roles of the Consultant

When helping other individuals, groups, organizations, or larger social systems, consultants behave in a number of roles that they judge to be appropriate for the client, the situation, and the helper's own style. What are these basic roles the consultant assumes in going about the helping process?

Argyris (1970) and Blake and Mouton (1976) clarify the consultant roles in terms of the intervention strategies used by the consultant. The intervention decisions are steered by the values and sensitivities of the consultant and the needs of the consultee.

Bennis (1973) identifies three roles for a change agent: training, consulting, and applied research. While not focusing solely on the consulting role, he emphasizes the roles of educator and fact finder.

In their monograph, Lawrence and Lorsch (1969) propose a threefold role for an OD specialist: educator, diagnostician, and consultant. They write:

> If an OD specialist is going to be effective at achieving both commitment to, and more sophisticated solutions for, organization development issues, he will have to clearly view his role as that of an educator and a diagnostician, as well as a consultant. That is, he will have to be able to develop techniques for identifying organization problems and analyzing their causes. He will have to be able to educate managers and other organization members in the use of concepts to conduct diagnoses and to plan action. Finally, he will have to act as a consultant in providing his own action proposals for the managers to consider. (p. 95)[1]

---

[1] From P. R. Lawrence and J. D. Lorsch, *Developing Organizations: Diagnosis and Action*. Reading, MA: Addison-Wesley, 1969, p. 95. Reprinted by permission of the publisher.

27

Menzel (1975) and Havelock (1973) add a fourth role of linker to the three indicated above. They present the linker function as the awareness of resources and the linking of the needs of the client and relevant resources.

In the provocative article, "Consultants and Detectives," Steele (1969) suggests that consultant roles are similar to those of fictional British detectives. Both roles share several attributes, as follows:

1. The temporary nature of involvement in a system;
2. The focus on gathering evidence and trying to solve the puzzles which it represents;
3. The potential for "dramatics";
4. The potential action orientation and the excitement it contains;
5. The stance of "expert" in behavioral science;
6. The stimulation of working on several "cases" at once. (p. 200)[2]

Steele points out several responsibilities that must be assumed by the consultant to prevent the aforementioned satisfactions from getting out of hand:

1. Promoting consciousness of self;
2. Avoiding incorporation into the client system;
3. Arranging for some collaborator or "sounding board" with whom to check perceptions, ideas, and feelings;
4. Using intuition as one means of generating ways to understand the situation;
5. Being wary of the tendency to lump people into the oversimplified categories of "good" and "bad." (p. 200)[3]

These varied observations make it difficult to define the helping process in terms of a set of specific roles for a consultant.

In a helpful model, Margulies and Raia (1972) divide consultative roles into "task oriented" and "process oriented" roles. Their concept is indicated in Figure 2.

As a result of our own experience and search, we have developed a *descriptive* model that presents the consultant's role along a *directive*

---

[2]Reproduced by special permission from *The Journal of Applied Behavioral Science*. "Consultants and Detectives," by Fred I. Steele, Vol. 5, No. 2, pp. 193-194, 200. Copyright 1969 NTL Institute for Applied Behavioral Science.

[3]See Footnote 2.

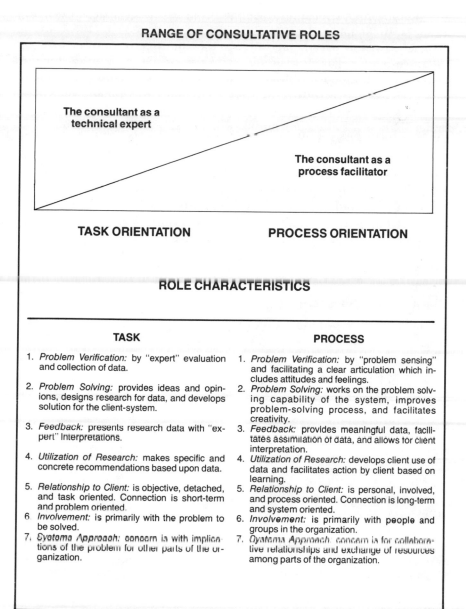

RANGE OF CONSULTATIVE ROLES

The consultant as a
technical expert

The consultant as a
process facilitator

TASK ORIENTATION   PROCESS ORIENTATION

ROLE CHARACTERISTICS

TASK	PROCESS
1. *Problem Verification:* by "expert" evaluation and collection of data.	1. *Problem Verification:* by "problem sensing" and facilitating a clear articulation which includes attitudes and feelings.
2. *Problem Solving:* provides ideas and opinions, designs research for data, and develops solution for the client-system.	2. *Problem Solving:* works on the problem solving capability of the system, improves problem-solving process, and facilitates creativity.
3. *Feedback:* presents research data with "expert" interpretations.	3. *Feedback:* provides meaningful data, facilitates assimilation of data, and allows for client interpretation.
4. *Utilization of Research:* makes specific and concrete recommendations based upon data.	4. *Utilization of Research:* develops client use of data and facilitates action by client based on learning.
5. *Relationship to Client:* is objective, detached, and task oriented. Connection is short-term and problem oriented.	5. *Relationship to Client:* is personal, involved, and process oriented. Connection is long-term and system oriented.
6. *Involvement:* is primarily with the problem to be solved.	6. *Involvement:* is primarily with people and groups in the organization.
7. *Systems Approach:* concern is with implications of the problem for other parts of the organization.	7. *Systems Approach:* concern is for collaborative relationships and exchange of resources among parts of the organization.

Figure 2. An organic consultative model
(From *Organization Development: Values, Processes, and Technology* by N. Margulies and A. Raia. Copyright 1972 by McGraw-Hill, Inc. Adapted by permission of McGraw-Hill Book Company.)

and *nondirective* continuum. Behavior varies in its degree of directiveness. In the more directive consultant role, the consultant assumes leadership and directs the activity. In the nondirective mode, the consultant provides data, for the client to use or not, as a guide for the client's self-initiated problem solving. These roles are not mutually exclusive but may manifest themselves in many ways at any stage in a particular client situation. We see these roles as spheres of competence rather than as a static continuum of isolated behavior. The model is presented in Figure 3.

In the past, the consultant role has been used in a nondirective mode, particularly by those in the clergy or counseling field, or as an expert function by engineers and other technical specialists who are called in by a client to solve a problem. Both of these functions, plus others, are proper and legitimate when done *appropriately* by a competent internal or external consultant or helping person.

ROLE DESCRIPTIONS

Consultant as Advocate

When the word *advocate* is mentioned among persons discussing consultants, a variety of verbal images is created. The consultant as an advocate may be seen as:

- A fighter
- A strong believer
- A provocateur
- One who is aggressive in attempting to influence others
- A person with convictions and values
- A person with guts
- A persuader
- An expert with a highly directive posture

Several common threads seem to weave their way through these perceptions of the consultant as an advocate. One is the idea of strength—the consultant as an advocate is seen as someone with potency and influence. A second thread is the idea of imposing one's ideas and values. The advocate-consultant is perceived as using an element of mobilizing force or a threat of consequences in his intervention strategy. The dictionary confirms at least part of these perceptions:

ad·vo·cate, one who defends, vindicates, or espouses a cause by argument; a persuader.

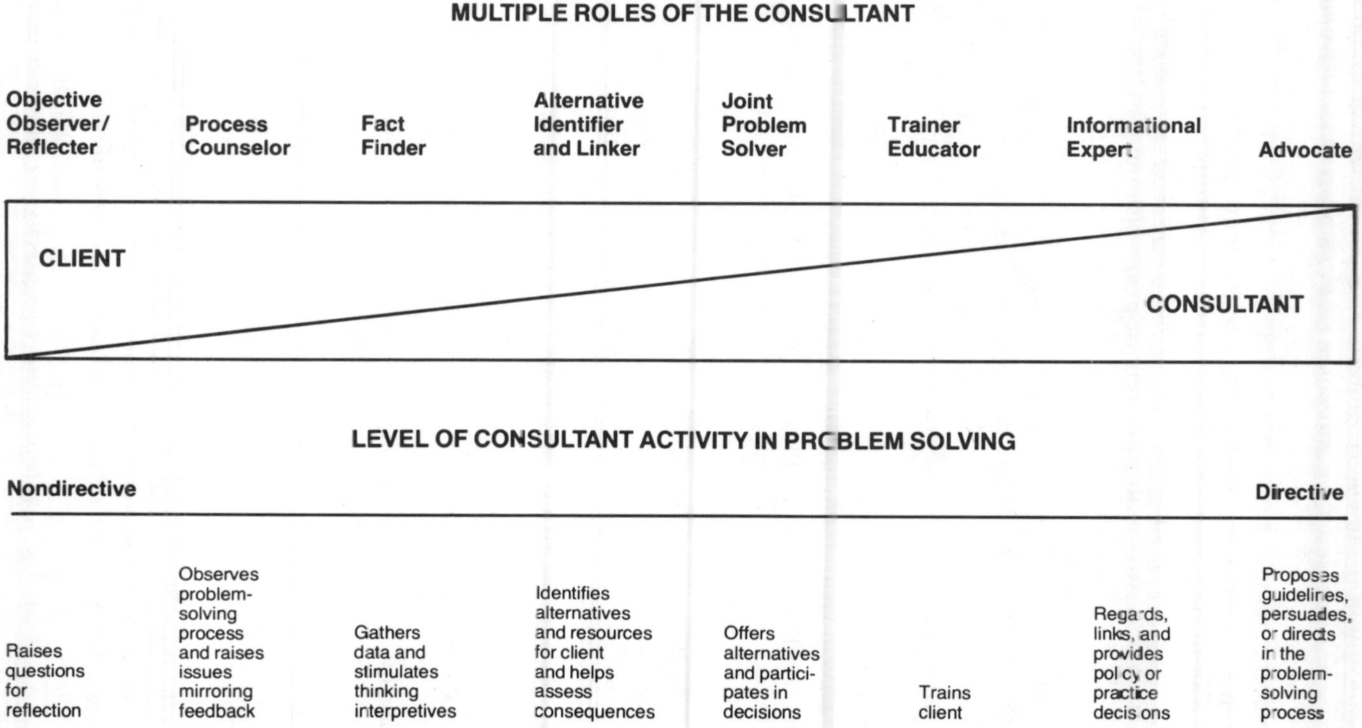

MULTIPLE ROLES OF THE CONSULTANT

CLIENT — CONSULTANT

Objective Observer/ Reflecter	Process Counselor	Fact Finder	Alternative Identifier and Linker	Joint Problem Solver	Trainer Educator	Informational Expert	Advocate
Raises questions for reflection	Observes problem-solving process and raises issues mirroring feedback	Gathers data and stimulates thinking interpretives	Identifies alternatives and resources for client and helps assess consequences	Offers alternatives and participates in decisions	Trains client	Regards, links, and provides policy or practice decisions	Proposes guidelines, persuades, or directs in the problem-solving process

LEVEL OF CONSULTANT ACTIVITY IN PROBLEM SOLVING

Nondirective   Directive

Figure 3. Description of the consultant's role on a directive and nondirective continuum

If the consultant is viewed in general as a person who attempts to help others solve problems, the advocate role can present some issues. It would seem that an advocate might "go around telling people what to do." Research into the nature of the helping relationship suggests that dependency on the helper is usually not in the long-range interests of the client. Clients must have an active role in the solution of their own problems. Since many consultants may not think it helpful, or even possible, to function without personal values, a dilemma exists. The consultant *has* values and wants to be of influence, but mere *push* is usually not helpful to the client.

One method of sorting out this situation is to make a distinction between the *content* and the *process* advocate.

- In the positional or content advocacy role, the consultant influences the client to choose particular goals or to accept particular values and actions.

- In the methodological or process advocacy role, the consultant influences the client to become active as a problem-solver and to use certain methods of problem solving—but is careful not to become an advocate for any particular solution (which would be positional advocacy).

The consultant who is a *content advocate* will attempt a conscious influence on choice of goals and means. For example, a consultant who acts as a content advocate might actively promote producing brown widgets rather than red widgets, or choosing computer systems over manual systems, or choosing particular curricular materials.

The consultant who is a *process advocate* will attempt a conscious influence on the methodology underlying the client's problem-solving behavior. For example, a process advocate might suggest an open meeting rather than a closed one, in order to increase trust in the system. In this sense, the advocate-consultant is less concerned with what is specifically said at the meeting than with the general method or approach to the meeting itself. Both these views of the advocate involve the *values* of the consultant. Both assume that the consultant will intervene in some way that exerts pressure on the system. However, the scope of the goals or values is quite different. The goals of the content advocate are rather specific, but those of the process advocate are broad and more flexible.

The consultant often plays an advocate's role, becoming an advocate of content or process, or some of both. The type of advocacy role that the consultant assumes is contingent on several factors, such as the consultant's personal goals, a minimal receptivity on the part of the client, and the interpersonal vs. technical nature of the task. The consultant considers the time frame, the risks, and alternative consequences. Although there may be more potential risk to the external advocates, they are also less owned by the client system and, consequently, can usually exert more influence on the system.

In a sense, it is not possible for a consultant to avoid being some type of advocate. By the consultant's very presence, he or she has influence on the client system. The question becomes more a decision about *what* the consultant will advocate and how the consultant will carry out this advocacy. For consultants who see themselves in a helping relationship with their clients, process advocacy becomes an overall feature of their approach, relating to all the other roles they take with a client system.

In summary, the choice of advocate behavior is derived from the helper's values and beliefs about the appropriate content and style of influence and its consequences.

Information Specialist

One of the roles of a consultant is that of information specialist. The more traditional role of a consultant is that of a specialist who, through his special knowledge, skill, and professional experience, is engaged as an internal or outside consultant to provide special-knowledge services. The client is mainly responsible for defining the problem and the objectives of the consultation, and the consultant assumes a directive role until the client is comfortable with the particular approach recommended. In some cases, consultants never move out of this role, as indicated by Steele (1969):

> I think the role of "expert" is a quite seductive one for the consultant—all the more so in behavioral science since the variables and their relationships are often quite fuzzy and complex. It can be quite personally gratifying to have others see me as someone who really "knows" what is going on or what should be done in a given situation. Besides personal gratification on the part of the consultant, another factor pushes him toward the stance of expert: the client's wish to see himself safely in the hands of an expert who is wise and able so that anxiety over present or future difficulties can be reduced. (pp. 193-194)[4]

Although the needs of both the consultant and the client may encourage this role of expert, the consultant should not follow this behavior pattern exclusively. In addition to the issue of increased

---

[4]See Footnote 2.

dependency, the exclusive expert role may lead to poor problem solving because of limited consideration of alternatives.

Some helpers feel that the role of content expert should be avoided by a consultant, but the role of process specialist is appropriate. Such a position is espoused by Schein (1969), who states that the:

> consultant should not withhold his expertise on matters of the learning process itself; but he should be very careful not to confuse being an expert on how to help an organization to learn with being an expert on the actual management problems which the organization is trying to solve. (p. 120)[5]

We believe there may be times when giving advice on both methodological and problem selection is appropriate. However, the use of this role must be selective and restrained. Everyone likes to give advice, but such advice is resisted if it is not offered at a particular time in the relationship, situation, and problem-solving process. Frequently, the consultant gives information early to help meet the immediate needs of the client. Later in the relationship, the consultant may act as a catalyst and procedural helper in implementing the recommendations that have been made.

Both the internal consultant and the external consultant may function as content specialists on the problems of the client or as process specialists on how to cope with a problem.

Trainer/Educator

Innovation consultation may require the use of periodic or continuous training and education within the client system. The consultant may be a designer of learning experiences or a direct teacher, using the skills of a designer, leader, and evaluator of the learning process.

The trainer/educator role of the consultant may be essential in designing and facilitating a learning process or an organization-change process. We have observed that the initiation of new organizational methods, such as management by objectives (MBO), program budget management systems, strategic planning, or management information systems, have often failed in their implementation because the consultant and organizational leaders did not give proper attention to the training process. If persons in the organization do not have skill in one-to-one relationships, interviewing, and on-the-job observation, the procedures and forms of an innovation such as MBO will not work.

---

[5] From E. H. Schein, *Process Consultation: Its Role in Organization Development*. Reading, MA: Addison-Wesley, 1969, p. 120. Reprinted by permission of the publisher.

The training role may be a part of a continuing consulting relationship. For example, one of us, in consulting with the president of a community college about his desire to develop a five-year plan for the college, served as an expert and joint planner. Following this phase of consultation, the consultant suggested a work conference, using the ITORP (Implementing the Organizational Renewal Process) *Organization Renewal Work Conference* modules, with ten administrators, ten students, ten trustees, and ten faculty members. The college president agreed, and the forty went away for a weekend conference.

During the last two sessions of the conference, which were designed for action planning and implementing, the group made fourteen recommendations for action. The president indicated that one fell in his area of responsibility, two were the responsibility of the trustees, one was the responsibility of the student council, one was referred to the faculty senate, and one went to the director of admissions. That left eight problem areas. The president and the group set up eight task forces to follow up those eight recommendations. The shortest task force lasted for three months and the longest for fourteen months. Within fifteen months, all fourteen recommendations had been acted on by the appointed person or groups.

This training/conference experience increased the participant's involvement, identified problem areas, and set in motion actions that led to the adoption of a five-year plan. Training in joint problem solving became a natural, flowing part of a two-year consultation process.

The trainer/educator role is one that is appropriate during a consultation when a particular learning process is indicated in order for the client system to acquire competency in certain areas. The consultant might consider some form of training function as part of the helping role when:

- An organization wants to develop its own strategy for self-development and self-confidence and encourage authentic interpersonal competence in its staff.
- A commitment has been made to re-educate staff members in human relations in order to unfreeze their attitudes and behavior.
- An organization wants to develop or cultivate the interpersonal skills of key individuals to increase the effectiveness of individual and group activities in problem solving.
- An organization wants to promote an adaptive style of interpersonal competence, focusing on the value and development of responsibility, esteem, and self-acceptance.
- The client needs to develop new job skills or enrich current jobs for better performance.

Some of the skills used by the consultant/trainer are:

- Assessing the training needs related to the problem;
- Developing and stating measurable objectives for learning experiences;
- Understanding the learning and change process;
- Designing a learning experience;
- Planning and designing educational events;
- Going beyond traditional training and using heuristic laboratory methods;
- Using multiple learning stimuli, including multimedia;
- Functioning as a group teacher or trainer;
- Helping others learn how to learn.

Yes, we believe that a consultant should be an experienced trainer/educator; we believe this to be a primary competency of any internal or external consultant. It is not the only role, but an important one in many helping situations.

Joint Problem Solver

The role of helper in problem solving involves complementing and collaborating with the client in all the perceptual, cognitive, emotional, and action processes needed to solve a problem. During the formulating and clarifying of a problem, the consultant helps maintain objectivity while stimulating ideas and interpretations. Additionally, the consultant can help isolate and define the basic factors that cause a problem and maintain it, or that could be activated to solve it. The consultant usually assists in weighing alternatives, sorting out the most critical causal relationships that may affect alternative solutions, and developing a course of action. In this role, the consultant is involved in the analysis and decision making as a *peer*. However, sometimes in conflict problems, the consultant may also assume the role of a third-party mediator.

Under the right circumstances, a consultant in this role brings to a client and to a situation important resources through the ability to:

- Perceive the situation more accurately;
- Provide a more inclusive perspective of the situation by testing the assumptions;
- Help define goals more clearly;
- Express and test alternatives;
- Provide a sense of reality;
- Confront sensitive areas;

- Save client time and resources;
- Reinforce commitments;
- Link existing resources to other resources;
- Catalyze action;
- Reduce a problem into manageable parts;
- Use and expand client resources.

These contributions clearly require receptivity from the client and role flexibility on the part of the consultant.

Identifier Of Alternatives And Linker To Resources

The value of a particular decision depends on its appropriateness for helping to attain a given set of objectives. When selecting an appropriate solution to a problem, several alternatives usually can be identified, along with their attendant risks. Either because of economics or other implications, the consultant should identify the alternatives with the client. The consultant must establish relevant criteria for assessing alternatives, developing cause-and-effect relationships for each alternative, along with the assessment of probable consequences.

In this helping relationship, the consultant functions not as a *participant* in the decision making itself, but as a *retriever* of the appropriate alternatives available to solve the problem and as a linker of the client to inside and outside resources. This particular helping role mixes two interrelated functions.

Some persons feel that the linking function is a separate role function. According to Havelock (1973), the linker is "someone who knows about resources, knows about people's needs, and knows how to bring client and resources together" (p.18). However, we consider linking to be a necessary part of the alternative-identification process, so that action is not limited by the resources of the client or the consultant. The good consultant does not limit the alternatives and resources to his own area of expertise. As French and Bell (1973) point out:

> In the future, organization development specialists must know much more about such matters (i.e., the task, technical and structural aspects and their interdependencies) and must establish linkages with practitioners in such fields as management science, personnel and industrial psychology, operations research, and industrial engineering in order to provide a broader range of options for organizational intervention. (p. 195)[6]

---

[6]From Wendell L. French and Cecil H. Bell, Jr., *Organization Development: Behavioral Science Interventions for Organization Improvement*, ©1973, p. 195. By permission of Prentice-Hall, Inc., Englewood Cliffs, New Jersey.

The consultant must be able to reveal to the client a wide range of options for action and helpful resources.

Fact Finder

Fact finding is an integral part of the consulting process, whether it be for developing a data base or for diagnosing intricate client problems. It is one of the most critical aspects of problem solving, and it often is the one that receives the least attention. This function requires development of criteria and guidelines to be used in the actual fact finding and related analysis, and includes the analysis and synthesis of the facts. Fact finding can be as simple as listening or as complex as a formal survey utilizing a number of computerized techniques. In this role, the consultant is functioning basically as a researcher.

The internal or external consultant should have at his or her command proven fact-finding techniques or data-collection methods. The ways in which an internal or external consultant gathers data or facts about a problem may vary. The internal consultant is part of the system and may be able to readily collect data bearing on the problem. The external consultant may not have such easy access, but may have the advantage of credible objectivity. In either case, there are five primary methods that can be employed in order to gather facts; they include the collection of data by:

1. Interviewing
2. Questionnaire
3. Observation
4. Analysis of records and documents
5. Administration and analysis of appropriate tests

Why is it important for a consultant, whether an internal or external consultant, to be a fact finder? First, fact finding can give the consultant valuable understanding of the client's processes, in addition to being a guide to the client's performance in meeting goals, schedules, and objectives. From these insights, the consultant and client can evaluate how well a change process is working and how well it has met or is meeting its problem-solving objectives.

Second, by collecting data with the client, the consultant is actually having an influence on the client system. Therefore, how one plans, implements, and collects the facts is an important consultative behavior. The consultant must know what data to look for, where and how to secure it in the least disruptive manner, and how to involve and motivate clients to become interested in the findings. The skill of planning and giving *data feedback* is an essential part of the fact-finding role.

As mentioned earlier, the consultant can help the client use five primary techniques to collect data. These range from indirect techniques, such as collecting data via questionnaire, to direct interviews in face-to-face situations. Interviewing can also occur in group situations. Sometimes the cross talk that occurs in group interviews can provide more data and insights than the individual interview. Often, the collection of data through observation and record analysis is a key source of fact finding. The consultant must know how and when to employ each technique, and secure the collaboration of the client.

Some of the key variables to consider when choosing a fact-finding method include the following:

1. *Time:* which technique will provide the most timely data?
2. *Costs:* what are the costs associated with collecting the data? The consultant should consider not only the costs in money, but in terms of time in human resources.
3. *Needs:* which technique best fits the current need of the client? Which method is most appropriate in terms of approach?
4. *Nature of the client:* what are the values of the client? Which technique is most appropriate for the client?

The collection of data, by whatever method, is an integral part of the consultant's job. The consultant must realize that in utilizing any one of the techniques, he will be intervening to some degree in the functioning of the client system, and he must know how much direct intervention the client system can tolerate. An ethical helper must take care to respect confidences and to protect the sources of information.

Process Counselor

Process work may be involved in *all* the roles of the helper, but there is a particular role for the consultant as a process specialist. Schein (1969) defines it as follows:

> Process consultation is a set of activities on the part of the consultant which help the client to better perceive, understand, and act upon process events which occur in the client's environment. (p. 9)[7]

Most significant is the definition of process consultation as a joint

---

[7]From E. H. Schein, *Process Consultation: Its Role in Organization Development*. Reading, MA: Addison-Wesley, 1969, p. 9. Reprinted by permission of the publisher.

diagnosis by the consultant and the client, with the intent of transferring to the client the skills necessary to continue such diagnosis.

The consultant's major focus is on the interpersonal and intergroup dynamics affecting the problem-solving process. Frequently, process consultation is closely allied with fact-finding activities using observation methods. The process consultant directly observes people in action and conducts interviews with management personnel from the president down; the purpose is to obtain facts and report the data to the client system in order to improve organizational relationships and processes. The process consultant must be able to effectively diagnose who and what is hindering organizational effectiveness and to report these observations to the appropriate person or persons in the organization.

The consultant works on developing joint client-consultant diagnostic skills for addressing specific and relevant problems, focusing on *how* things are done rather than what tests are performed. He helps the client to integrate interpersonal and group skills and events with task-oriented activities and to support the improvement of relationships.

Objective Observer/Reflector

The objective role of reflector/observer is a series of consultant activities directed at stimulating the client toward some insights into growth, a discovery of better methods, a look at long-range change, and greater independence.

This is the most nondirective consulting approach. The consultant communicates none of his own beliefs and ideas to the client and is not responsible for the work or the outcome. The client is responsible for the direction chosen and reaches decisions by himself.

When operating as a reflector, the consultant asks reflective questions that help the client to clarify and confront the problems and to make decisions. The consultant may also paraphrase, probe, and be empathic, experiencing with his client the blocks that initially provoked the problem. In this role, the consultant finds himself being a philosopher—taking a long-range view.

The actions that take place in this role are similar to those of process counselor, but some of the emphasis is different. An interesting question to explore is the relationship of the consultant roles to client decisions. Typically, both extremes of the role spectrum do not terminate until a decision has been reached—by the consultant, in the case of the advocate, and by the client, in the case of the reflector/observer.

The role of reflector/observer requires some trade-offs that should be considered when using this approach. One trade-off involves, on one side, the consultant's commitment of time and flexibility, a the other side, the client's acceptance and trust of the consultant.

Two additional points can be made about the nondirective reflector role:

1. When performing as the reflector/observer, the consultant must continue the role until the client reaches a decision. This precludes some flexibility in the consultant's time with the client.

2. This form of consultation tends to increase the levels of frustration within the client system. Although this is the heightened level of frustration that usually precedes increased self-awareness, it may be unacceptable to a business organization or to an executive in a demanding environment.

This role, like all the others, is usually not performed in an unadulterated form; most consultants use multiple roles in working with a client.

CRITERIA FOR CONSULTANT ROLE SELECTION

This section examines the variables that determine the consultant's choice of role for a particular client situation and phase of the consulting relationship. We have made it clear that (a) there are numerous consultant roles that can be interpreted in many ways; and (b) the role assumed by the consultant may vary from moment to moment. To speak of roles as separate and distinct is a distortion. More to the point is the question of which role is predominant at any given moment or for the longest period of time.

One might ask, "To what degree does a consultant make a conscious decision about the role he or she will assume?" We believe that the consultant reacts to a situation with his or her whole being and with behavior that is determined less by a process of deliberate decision making than by a complex of trained reactions and experiential responses, some of which are unexplainable. But in the process of learning consultation, reflection about such distinctions and decisions is important.

Our criteria for role choice are more descriptive than prescriptive, resulting from what we have seen and felt. Our descriptions are not intended to convey a sense of "this is the right thing to do." Our goal for the consultant is effectiveness, and to the degree that our role-choice criteria are effective for the consultant-practitioner, then that purpose has been achieved.

We have found no way to measure with confidence which factors are key determinants in the consultant's role selection. More often than not, the literature on the subject describes personal experience and attempts to relate that experience to universal constants. The following factors appear to be among the most important in role selection. They are not the only ones, nor even the best, but we believe them to be the most common in practice.

The Nature of the Contract

The mutual understanding between the consultant and the client system concerning their professional relationship is their *contract*. Sometimes it is a written document, sometimes an oral agreement. Whatever form it takes, it becomes a *psychological contract*. Difficulty in coping with the contract can arise from its endless variations, existing in the minds of involved individuals.

Not only does the consultation deal with expectations but also with changing perceptions and the modifications brought about by interaction. The contract is a process because change is inherent in the nature of human relationships and because the presence of a new force (the consultant) changes the very nature of the problem to be attacked.

The contract, as it is perceived by the client and consultant, probably sets the initial hierarchy of consultant roles. The first form of the contract is established either during the entry or before it. The contract will change with each development that follows, but how it changes will be largely determined by its initial form. To the degree that the contract is structured and specific, the role of the consultant will be relatively unchanging (barring a new contract). To the degree that the contract is general and unstructured, the role of the consultant may vary continually.

Goals

Goals can also be seen as a process. Not only do the consultant and the members of the client system begin with multiple goals, but they change them and reorder their priorities from time to time. Again, as the presence of the consultant affects the perceptions and operations of that system, it also has impact on the goals of the client system.

A third-party role is relevant for a consultant who is involved with resolving an intergroup conflict. But if the two groups are to assume responsibility, then the role of trainer/educator would be relevant for helping them to develop conflict-resolution skills.

Norms and Standards of the Client System and the Consultant

By norms and standards, we mean the full spectrum of values from etiquette to morals and life style. Unlike the consulting contract, norms and standards resist change. Although they, too, are processes, norms and standards tend to change more slowly as the individual and the client system age. In fact, one of the frequent unheralded tasks of the consultant—particularly the process consultant—is to change the value systems of the client.

Generally, the narrower the norms and standards of the client system, the more constricted the role of the consultant. This is true as long as (1) the norms and standards tend to be consistent from one member of the client system to the next, and (2) the consultant does not choose the tactic of changing the client system by confronting it with an unexpected role.

To the degree that the norms and standards of the client system and the consultant differ, the consultant will tend more toward the directive end of the directive-nondirective scale. Under these conditions, the consultant may use other role orientations to support that of the advocate in trying to secure congruence with the client.

Personal Limitations and Inclinations of the Consultant

We believe that the determining factors in the consultant's choice of roles are his natural predelictions and competencies. Personal style, as Walton (1969) points out, strongly conditions the roles and interventions of the consultant. Interpersonal competence, including self-awareness, is the first skill Beckhard (1969) lists as a requirement for the OD consultant. Self-awareness that leads to interpersonal competence implies an acceptance of one's limitations. Therefore, role choice is likely to be affected by the consultant's view of the role in which he or she feels most effective and comfortable. The greater the versatility and the broader the role repertoire of the consultant, the more likely he or she is to succeed in a variety of settings.

What Worked Before

All people are victims of *set*—that proclivity of the mind to reuse what has worked before. Consultants are no exceptions. As long as the nature of the client group tends to remain the same from one consulting assignment to the next, it is likely that the consultant will use the same roles. But to be able to deal with varied client systems, the consultant should be able to recognize this tendency toward set and adapt to changing contexts.

Internal and External

It is our feeling that a consultant's role choice tends to be more and more related to the degree that he or she is an integral member of the client system. For example, the consultant who is subordinate to the same boss as the group he or she is working with frequently will be forced into the role of policeman or watchdog. This is less likely to be true for someone from another part of the organization. Of course, we know of many exceptions to this rule, but it is more often true than not.

Role expectations for internal consultants are limited insofar as they are not independent agents and their functions within organizations are specified. Aside from encountering resentment for intervening, the internal consultant must face preconceived notions of how much he or she will tell the boss and what specific changes will be effected.

Because of these circumstances, there seem to be two trends for the internal consultant. One is for the internal consultant to become more and more external, for example, separating the consulting staff from the company and making it an independent concern. The other trend is for the consultant to become more and more constrained in his role and sphere of operation.

Events

Events external to the consultation process can have a profound impact on the client system and/or the consultant and cause the consultant to change his role. The birth of a child, the beginning of a war, a change in organizational leadership, race riots, or fluctuations in the stock market can change the complexion of the client system or the outlook of the consultant to the point that a change in roles occurs.

Earlier in this chapter, we presented a model that linked role selection with a degree of directiveness-nondirectiveness. That model, like all others attempting to depict human situations, has limited utility and validity; it is true and accurate part of the time. Now, we ask the reader to see role selection as a process determined by a number of other processes, some of which have been described. As in any system of interrelated processes, the selection of one role causes changes in the determining processes themselves, which in turn modify the role selection, and so on. Each of the processes affects all others. Because of its complexity, we have been unable to construct a model of this process. But, if the behavior of the consultant is perceived as a process within a process, then the realities of consultation in action have been communicated.

Chapter 4
Intervention Decisions and Actions: Dilemmas, Strategies, and Learning

It is an exciting challenge to find ways of developing and using the self effectively as a problem-solving resource and as a sensitive tool in all the roles and phases of consultation.

To be an effective helper requires making many decisions about whether help is needed, how and when to be helpful, and what might be an appropriate source of help. The sensitive consultant considers many alternatives in making such decisions and, consequently, faces many dilemmas. With increased sensitivity, consultants are aware of more decision potentialities, deal with more momentary dilemmas, and guide their decisions and actions more to meet the needs of those they are helping.

This chapter is focused on the variety of opportunities the consultant has for considering alternatives, making decisions, and using skills to actualize the decisions competently. This last point is explored more fully in Chapter 7.

The first part of this chapter examines several core decision-making areas of consulting, in which important dilemmas must be dealt with, such as the consultant's diagnostic orientation, degree of collaboration with the client, resource-mobilization strategy, and experimental or risk-taking orientation.

The second part of the chapter classifies types of intervention or clusters of intervention decisions that comprise a partial inventory of decision dilemmas for consultants.

We then relate this framework to our phases of consultation by identifying some of the typical dilemmas of intervention decision making that occur in the different phases.

Finally, we look at the challenge of linking decisions with skillful actions, and at some ways to improve one's skills in making decisions and taking action.

DIAGNOSTIC INTERVENTIONS AND DILEMMAS

In the consultant role, it often is important to think of oneself as a busy diagnostic center—collecting data from clients, from the demands and characteristics of the situation, from past experience and training, and from one's own feelings, values, and concepts. We ask many questions to secure necessary data on the client system. The following are a few of the questions that are a part of an active diagnostic process.

- How well is the client system functioning?
- What are some hunches about what is causing it to behave the way it does?
- How can we check our hunches?
- How ready is it to make data about itself available?
- Based on the facts, what are the implications for change?
- What motivations are there for readiness or resistance to change efforts?

In sensitivity training with two different groups, we discovered that developing a repertoire of alternatives was a key element of diagnostic sensitivity. Individuals who generated the most hunches about the causes of behavior, or who suggested the most number of possible implications for the behavior of others, also proved to make the highest quality decisions. It seemed clear that one of the most important resources for making competent or correct decisions was being able to identify a variety of alternatives.

But having alternatives is only part of the personal resources that are needed. It is also necessary to have a framework of values or criteria for making choices between alternatives. My sensitivity to a client's behavior, such as perceiving that a client resists change in his or her authoritarian supervisory style, can provide some good hunches. But I also need criteria guiding me to accept those alternatives that favor collaboration, support, and acceptance, and to reject those alternatives that would make the client feel guilty, defensive, or angry. Without such evaluation, my intervention decision might be very inappropriate, although my ideas might be extensive.

Rosenberg (1951) revealed the following interesting dilemmas:

- A consultant who develops deep empathy for the client generates fewer causal hypotheses about the client's needs and motivations;
- The consultant who identifies deeply with the client and becomes an advocate for the client is often a poorer resource of help. This consultant is unable to generate alternative ideas for

problem-solving action and has more limited value criteria for choosing appropriate ways of helping.

Here are three other important decision-making dilemmas that challenge consultants as they develop and utilize their diagnostic resources:

1. One challenging decision is how much time and energy to invest in an initial fact-finding or diagnostic phase, as contrasted to moving quickly into some pilot actions and developing diagnostic information from observations of what happens.

2. A second challenge is to decide how much the client or client group should be involved in the actual fact-finding activities, as contrasted with the use of experts who have more technical tools and skills. The deeper data collected by experts is often rejected and resisted by the client because there has been no development of ownership and validity of the data. This can be compared to the action-research model, which involves the client system in defining the inquiry questions, developing the procedures to be used, and helping to collect and process the information.

3. A third dilemma arises with the question of how much of the data should be shared and when. It is possible to overload the client, or to create undue fear and anxiety in an early stage of the helping process. On the other hand, only through sharing data can the understanding of the change effort and the motivation to become involved in it develop.

ORIENTATION TOWARD COLLABORATION

Who is my contract with? Who am I working for and with? The question of who the client system really is and how to relate to him, her, or them is often one of the most puzzling areas in consultation. Frequently, consultants find themselves relating too exclusively to the top executive or the initiator of the contract, when, in order to be effective, they should be relating to and regarding a total staff unit, or some other population, as the client system.

Often, the consultant must deal with the important and puzzling question of how to relate to one or more insiders as part of an ad hoc change-agent team, without creating difficulties with the rest of the system because of this special working relationship. Another dilemma the consultant faces is deciding to what degree to be an expert and an advocate of certain goals, procedures, and methods and to what degree to be a nondirective facilitator and supporter of the client system's mobilization of its own resources and goals.

RISK TAKING

Asking for help and working with a consultant sets up the implication and expectation that some new experiences and activities are in the offing. This prospect activates insecurity and caution about departing from the tried and true. Consequently, the consultant is almost always faced with a series of questions about the appropriate degree of risk taking. The problem becomes how to reduce the client's stress and defensiveness and still introduce enough change to make a difference.

A continuing dilemma is finding a balance or a mix of interventions that stimulate significant change effort and that support the client system as it participates in problem-solving activities to modify its functioning and its environment.

ORIENTATION TOWARD RESOURCE IDENTIFICATION AND UTILIZATION

At some point with almost every client, a consultant must face the following questions: Can I offer what they need now or later? Are other resources needed also? Will the client be disappointed with me if I clarify areas of inadequacy in my competencies and resources? How do I feel about suggesting that other sources of help are needed to complement me or to replace me? We believe all consultants need practice in working on these questions, with themselves and with their clients.

SOME DECISIONS ABOUT INTERVENTIONS, CONTEXT, AND TIMING

Consultants tend to get so focused on questions of what to do and say in their interactions with clients that they forget other intervention decisions concerning the context, the timing, and the methodology of offering help. There are four such topics that we believe to be important:

1. *Should the intervention be direct and face-to-face, or should it be performed through some other medium?*

Over the years in our consultation practice, we have discovered an increasing variety of situations in which the use of written memoranda and telephone calls seems superior to the greater time and energy expended in face-to-face interaction. The writing of a memorandum to a client can organize and clarify ideas, and the reading of the memo allows the client to do some thinking and reacting before a face-to-face session. An exchange of memos often is a very effective preliminary preparation for a conference. Using the telephone to make queries or to offer support has great advantages, particularly after a face-to-face relationship has been established. The consultant may have a face-to-face relationship with one person or with a small number of key persons who serve as links to the total client system. This saves the time, energy, and money that would be required to have a direct relationship with all parts of the system.

2. Focal Point of the Interventions

When considering focuses for our interventions, we have to make a choice between three possibilities:

1. An individual in his or her intrapersonal dynamics;
2. Interpersonal relationships and cliques, subgroups, or clusters within the client system;
3. The total system, organization, or collectivity.

Redel (1941) developed a principle in working with teachers that went something like this: one should not intervene to influence an individual member of the group unless the effect is at least neutral, if not positive, for the total group, and one should not intervene to influence the total group unless the impact will be at least neutral, if not positive, for each individual in the group. In our decision making, therefore, we think about both the appropriate level of intervention and the potential side effects.

3. To Act or Not To Act?

Part of our work with consultants involves practice in making decisions concerning interventions. In one of the most interesting exercises, each consultant records those points in an interaction in which he or she is tempted to intervene but decides not to.

A review of these decisions usually indicates that some of them were important lost opportunities, passed by because of a lack of ability to generate alternatives and to choose between them. But it seems clear that at other times, the consultant was wise to say and do nothing, having sensed that an intervention might inhibit the client's work, be timed poorly because of nonreadiness, or do work for the client that the client would like to initiate later, if given the time.

We believe the deliberate decision not to intervene is an important part of intervention decision making; it should be sharply differentiated from the consultant's neglect or avoidance of decisions he or she is not able or ready to make.

4. *Proactive or Reactive?*

One of the most critical decision dilemmas in working with client systems is the degree to which the consultant should be a proactive initiator of interventions or a responder to the problem-solving efforts and initiatives of the client.

There is a broad range of practice between (1) the relatively non-directive responder and supportive encourager of the activities of the client, and (2) the enthusiastic advocate and active initiator of interpretations, methods, and activities. It is our belief that all consultants must clarify for themselves the values and styles they use in this area of decision making.

WORK FOCUSES OF INTERVENTION DECISION AND ACTIONS

While working to improve our own consulting practice, we have utilized two frameworks to identify and classify intervention decisions and to become more sensitive to important decision dilemmas and their alternative solutions. Although they overlap somewhat, we have found both frameworks helpful. The first framework is oriented toward classifying the different focal points of consultative work, within which intervention decisions tend to cluster. The second framework utilizes the phases of consultation that were presented in Chapter 2.

Five Areas of Consultative Interventions

HELPING WITH TASK WORK

The consultant can intervene by helping the client work through the essential phases of problem solving and come out with action. Actually, the-consultant is involved with questions of *what* and *how*, such as helping the client to:

- Determine and clarify the job that needs to be done;
- Decide what tools and methods are most appropriate for each kind of task.

HELPING WITH PROCESS WORK

Productivity in work depends to a high degree on the effective use of procedures and relationships. Typically, very little attention is paid to the work problems that may be caused by insensitive interpersonal relationships and unsatisfactory group procedures. The consultant must determine how to help people to examine the way they are working together and to identify possible approaches to improving their working relationships. A second consulting process involves the client and consultant in looking at their working relationship, identifying issues of relationship, and developing ways to deal with these issues.

VALUE ORIENTATION WORK

The questions of *What?* and *How?* must always be accompanied by the question *Why?*. In typical work with a client, the consultant deals with issues, questions, and decisions regarding two kinds of value clarification and articulation. First, the consultant helps the client clarify possible goals and work through the rationale for choosing between them or giving some of them priority over others. .

The second kind of value orientation work is the developing of criteria for selecting among alternative ways of implementing the goals. Consultants often find themselves struggling with whether they have the right or responsibility to advocate their own value positions with their clients or whether they should place priority on helping the clients discover and articulate their own values.

WORKING ON RESOURCES

When working with clients on resources, the consultant usually focuses on three questions: What is needed? Where can it be found? How can it be used?

There is a strong tendency on the part of both clients and consultants to do the best they can with what they have at hand. Their eager problem-solving efforts may work against the reflective review that is needed to assess the kinds of resources that might be needed and desirable. And the information and skills that are needed to do a good job of searching for resources often are lacking or neglected. An even more serious issue exists when a variety of resources are compiled, but without a specific design for utilizing them to arrive at decisions and action plans.

As indicated earlier, a consultant sometimes must decide whether to appear less important and less expert by revealing the need for and the existence of other resources. We believe that designing and motivating effective use of resources is one of the most important and neglected areas of consultation.

ASSESSMENT WORK

One kind of consultant intervention involves helping the client to (1) define the progressive steps toward a goal, (2) determine ways of identifying progress toward the goal, and (3) utilize the evidence to celebrate progress and revise the direction of effort.

A second kind of help is with the selection or creation of evaluation tools. Tools are needed for collecting data to demonstrate and report accountability and to provide the information for revision of the next round of goals and action.

Client motivation lags and activity momentum dies without clearly identified steps toward goals and procedures for celebrating progress and for involving the appropriate people in such celebration.

Along with their clients, consultants tend to keep an eye on long-range goals and images of perfection. This leads to an awareness of a discrepancy between perfection and "where we are" (images of imperfection) and to feelings of depression and frustration.

In addition to meeting the more typical challenges of helping the client set up procedures for evaluation and reporting, it is important for the consultant to help the client achieve a step-by-step orientation toward progress and celebration.

A Partial Inventory of Decisions in Each Phase of Consultation

In Chapter 2, we explored six phases of the consultation process and identified several focuses of work in the consultant's relationship with clients. Here we begin a check list of critical decisions that consultants typically face in each consultative phase. This listing is certainly not complete, but the consultant can add to it with use.

PHASE 1. INITIAL CONTACT AND ENTRY

Critical Intervention Questions

1. How can I legitimize for clients their sharing of pain, problems, and sense of failure without also stimulating their defensiveness?

2. How can I ask probing questions and not mobilize feelings of irritation and hostility toward me?

3. How can I listen to and encourage the unloading of problems without appearing to accept the projections of blame and the attributions of causation of the exposed problems?

4. How can I demonstrate expertness and establish my credibility as a potential source of help without creating dependency and an expectation that I will solve the problem?

5. How can I explain readiness to work on change without appearing to assume (before diagnosis) that a lot of change is going to be needed?

6. How can I bring up and explore questions of compatibility without sounding too clinical, doubtful, or demanding?

7. How can my relevant experience and training be communicated without sounding like a sales pitch?

8. How can I be reassuring without being interpreted as saying the problem is minor or can be easily and quickly solved?

PHASE 2. FORMULATING A CONTRACT, ESTABLISHING A WORKING
        RELATIONSHIP

Critical Intervention Questions

1. How can I explore potential traps and misunderstandings with clients without appearing negative or disturbing?

2. How can I strike a balance between making clients' responsibilities and commitments seem too heavy (at this early stage) and letting them make false assumptions about the amount of work that will be expected by the consultant?

3. How can I find some ways to test compatibility and skills of collaboration without entering into some irreversible commitments?

4. How can I be clear about the level of my commitment of time and energy without appearing to sell myself or have inflexible standards?

5. How can I clarify some limitations of my resources without creating loss of confidence in me?

6. How can I realistically communicate my available time and energy without discouraging the client?

7. How can I work for involvement of appropriate parts of the system without antagonizing the ingroup?

8. How can I stretch the necessary time perspective of the contract without appearing to promote more work for myself?

9. How can I write the commitment about the participation of top management without creating defensiveness and gameplaying?

10. How can financial terms be definite and yet flexible in response to changes in conditions, e.g., new critical problems discovered, basic conflicts to be handled?

11. How can we define outcomes and accountability to be derived without creating traps and limitations?

12. How can division of labor be defined without too much rigidity and without scaring people?

PHASE 3. PROBLEM IDENTIFICATION AND DIAGNOSIS

Critical Intervention Questions

1. How can I get people to open up and question their assumptions about the causes of their problems?
2. How can I get them to accept the need for objective fact finding to supplement their own data assumptions?
3. How can I introduce perspective about the time that is needed without discouraging them?
4. How can I obtain their appropriate understanding and commitment of the time and energy that will be required of them?
5. How can I involve them enough in the diagnostic data-collection process for them to feel ownership of the data and accept its validity?
6. How can I arrange for the appropriate parts of the client system to review the data and draw implications for action?
7. How can I focus on data about need and readiness for change, rather than simply working on causes of the pain or the problem?

PHASE 4. GOAL SETTING AND PLANNING

Critical Intervention Questions

1. How can I create a psychological readiness in people to think into the future and freely imagine alternative futures?
2. How can I free them enough from inhibiting assumptions about adjusting, predicting, and feasibility to project a *desired* future based on their values?
3. How can I prevent them from choosing goals before they have tested alternatives for probable consequences?
4. How can I confront the tendency to involve too few members of the system in goal setting and planning?
5. How can I press for concreteness and measurability in goal statements without evoking a negative reaction?
6. How can I stimulate interest in step-by-step goal planning in place of a preoccupation only with big, long-term perspectives?
7. How can I support planning for evaluation as part of planning for implementation?
8. How can I help with reality testing of plans?
9. How can I help clients to explore the possible side effects and traps that are part of planning?

10. How can I push for personnel commitments of time, effort, and acceptance of deadlines without creating resistance and flight?

11. How can I stimulate clients to consider the need for and use of resources beyond themselves?

12. How can I plan for my withdrawal and the development of internal resources to replace my functions?

PHASE 5.   CONVERTING PLANS INTO ACTION

Critical Intervention Questions

1. How can I present to clients the necessity and value of action rehearsal so that it will be accepted?

2. How can I present and demonstrate the value of skill training?

3. How can I demonstrate and communicate the details of effective involvement, briefing techniques, and preparation for all implementation actions as replacements for the assumptions that good intentions and acceptance of goals are adequate?

4. How can I confront the weakness of an authoritative strategy with a process based on voluntary involvement?

5. How can I deal with the dependency of clients who want me to use my expertness to produce the action?

6. How can I introduce procedures for obtaining feedback on each action step and for using the data?

7. How can I support the use of other resources as an evidence of strength rather than weakness?

8. How can I introduce and support celebration of milestones of progress?

9. How can I help those who are taking action to understand the idea and the use of support systems and to use each other for support, reinforcement, and debriefing?

10. How can I support the commitment to document the action and the consequences?

PHASE 6.   CONTRACT COMPLETION: CONTINUITY AND SUPPORT

Critical Intervention Questions

1. How can I deal objectively with my own conflicting inclinations to see "all the help the clients still need" and also to move on to do "new and exciting things"?

2. How can I involve the client in setting goals that increase self-direction and internal support?

3. How can I make appropriate commitments for periodic support as needed?

4. How can I confront and support the need for specific deadlines on progress checkpoints, the need for renewal, and other items?

5. How can we find ways to provide support from a distance?

6. How can I support continuing plans for documentation and evaluation?

7. How can I support plans for continuing internal personnel development and internal change-agent functions?

8. How can I help to clarify the client's understanding of ongoing and potential needs for external help and appropriate procedures for securing such help?

9. How can we appropriately celebrate the completion of our contract?

LINKING INTERVENTION DECISIONS TO SKILLFUL ACTION

It is possible for a consultant to develop great sensitivity and skill in making diagnostic and intervention decisions, but still be ineffective as an intervener and helper. To be an effective actualizer of one's decisions requires behavioral skills. Without behavioral competency, a consultant can provide an ineffective representation of very sophisticated concepts and intentions. In the next chapter, we explore the skill repertoire of the competent consultant and suggest some ways to acquire this competence.

It is also true that consultants with perfectly adequate skills sometimes do not actualize their plans and intentions because they fail to take the risk of behavioral commitment. Most of us have experienced this phenomenon within ourselves. Some frequent reasons for the large gap between good intentions and behavioral output are a sense that others lack readiness for support, a prediction of risky consequences, and a feeling that the consequences of our actions will require more commitments than we want to make.

Chapter 5
Ethical Dilemmas and Guidelines for Consultants

Achieving personal and group guidelines and commitments for ethical behavior is crucial to the competence of a consultant. In this chapter, we examine the ethics of giving help, look at selected ethical dilemmas, and present some guidelines for behaving ethically as a consultant.

We want to develop awareness of the complexity of several ethical dilemmas. These dilemmas include the intrusion of preconceived images of the consultant-client relationship, dangers in the manipulation of human behavior, and the semantic contribution to conceptual confusion.

In any area of helping, the consultant occupies a position of trust and, therefore, the ethical aspects of his or her work and relationships occupy a significant place in the discussion of the consulting process. The work of all professional helpers requires the constant exercise of discretion and judgment. Their clients may not be qualified to appraise the quality of service being offered or the risks involved and, therefore, may have to rely for support and protection on the helper's standards of conduct and on the network of professional peers. The client is justified in expecting certain standards of conduct, and can derive confidence from knowing that a code of professional behavior will help to protect him.

Shay (1965) views ethics as

> standards of professional conduct and practice which stem from the nature of the profession. They are consistent with the profession's purposes and

We acknowledge the assistance of two persons, Paul R. Holland and Jane Schmithorst, who were helpful in our search of the literature on professional ethics.

57

functions in society and are generally considered to be the best ways of applying the knowledge and skills peculiar to it. (p. 13)[1]

According to Shay, ethics represent the attitudes, principles, and approaches that:

1. Contribute to the success of the professional's special work;
2. Make for equitable and satisfactory client relationships;
3. Relate his profession properly to the part of society which it serves. (p. 13)[2]

Since codes of professional ethics and practices are corollaries of professions, and since professional status is largely a consequence of them, what is generally meant by a profession should be noted. The Association of Consulting Management Engineers (1966) defines it as

> an occupation requiring extensive preliminary intellectual training, pursued for others and not merely one's self, and accepting as the measure of achievement one's contribution to society rather than individual financial reward. (p. 4)

In all the standard definitions of professions there are elements of dedication, of giving one's ethical position a place of extreme importance, of taking pride in applying one's knowledge and skills, and of functioning with integrity. In a field as complex and varied as consulting, ethical practice implies far more than simply profiting from the past mistakes of the profession. It demands a willingness to be alert to novel situations and to respond to them as they develop.

THE PROFESSIONAL

Shay (1965) defines the characteristics of a professional in any profession as being:

1. Knowledge of the profession, its philosophy, principles, and practices;
2. A continuing discipline of study and responsibility for assisting in the advancement and dissemination of professional knowledge;
3. A standard of conduct governing the relationships of the practitioners with prospective clients, clients, colleagues, members of allied professions, and the public;

---

[1] From Phillip W. Shay, "Ethics and Professional Practices in Management Consulting," in the *Advancement Management Journal*, 1965, 30(1), pp. 13-14.

[2] See Footnote 1.

4. A motive of service, as distinguished from primary preoccupation with making profit;

5. Professional pride—the belief on the part of the practitioner in the worthiness of his calling, and the influence this conviction has on guiding his actions. (p. 14)[3]

Basic postures, therefore, that allow a person to function effectively in a professional role are:

1. Acquiring the knowledge and learning the disciplines of the profession;

2. Learning to apply professional knowledge and skills effectively;

3. Always putting client interests ahead of personal or own-group interests;

4. Maintaining high standards for serving clients;

5. Behaving at all times with a professional bearing.

These statements establish the basic responsibility of developing and utilizing ethical guidelines for decision making and behavior in any consulting relationship and role.

We believe that readers who are interested in being effective helpers, but who do not think of themselves as members of a particular profession, will find it helpful to think of their efforts as "professionalizing" themselves as helpers.

SOURCES OF ETHICAL GUIDELINES

Persons who have had little experience in consulting may wonder why it is not a simple matter to conduct all professional dealings in accordance with the highest ethical standards. The difference between the proper and improper should be clear enough. But it is not that simple. All too frequently, the consultant faces decisions that involve ethical questions not easily resolved. Some consultants may find themselves working in areas where ethical standards are vague and ambiguous. In many instances, the consultant must walk a decision making tightrope, trying to balance fairly the sometimes conflicting interests of all those with whom he or she is professionally associated.

As a professional practitioner, the consultant is a maker of value judgments. Consulting involves activities in which choices must be made between alternative courses of action. When choosing between possible alternatives, a consultant is making a choice between two or

---

[3] See Footnote 1.

more values, and making such a choice often involves an ethical decision. Value judgments are an intrinsic and integral part of the consulting process.

The consultant makes some value judgments in a social context for which the larger society has already determined the most appropriate value choices. These do's and don'ts are enshrined in legal codes of prescriptions and prohibitions. Consequently, the guidelines for consulting decisions and behavior are sometimes found either in law or institutional procedures.

This level of consulting guidelines is what philosophers call normative ethics. A particular behavior is good or right if it is consistent with the accepted norm. As long as the consultant is content to accept the given norm, he or she can make value decisions with relative ease. "He is culture-bound and happy in its claims" (Golightly, 1971).

Valuation becomes painful when the consultant is no longer content with the provisions of existing law and institutional guidelines or when the issues are not covered by precedents and norms. How can a consultant know that a given idea, recommendation, or policy is right or that a proposed change is better unless he or she knows what *right* and *good* mean?

How do statements of value differ from statements of fact, and can values be verified in the same way as facts? Values arise out of human beliefs and desires. People establish goals or end values, and they experiment with means to achieve their goals, creating a continuum of ends and means that are subjected to norms about appropriate behaviors. These norms are continually tested in the experiential world. When the norms work, people keep them, and when they do not work, people are motivated to revise or discard them. Taking a rigid moralistic stance toward values often short circuits the circular process whereby the consequences of one's actions lead one back to a re-examination of our beliefs and motives.

According to Fletcher (1968), there are basically only three alternate routes or approaches to follow in making ethical decisions. They are (1) the legalistic, (2) the lawless or unprincipled approach, and (3) the situational.

In the legalistic approach, one enters into every decision-making situation with a whole code of preformulated rules and regulations. The lawless approach would have one entering into a decision-making situation armed with no principles or maxims whatsoever, except perhaps self-interest. The situational-ethical approach lies between these two. Since every situation is unique, one must rely on the situation itself, then and there, to provide its clues for the creation of an ethical decision. With this approach, one enters into every consulting situation equipped with the ethical maxims developed previously from experiencing somewhat similar situations.

Central to the use of ethical guidelines in most consulting situations is an awareness that circumstances alter cases. The person using situational ethics is willing to make full and respectful use of principles, treating them as maxims but not as laws. There is no real quarrel here between situational ethics and an ethics of principles, unless the principles become hardened into laws or regulations.

Ethics deals with human relations, and situational ethics is concerned with people, not codes. A common objection to situational ethics is that it calls for more self-discipline in commitment to values than most people are able to mobilize.

The multiple pressures and rapid changes that have characterized the era following World War II have increased the frequency and intensity of the value dilemmas of society and of consulting relationships. This increased conflict among values contributes to a general attitude of questioning traditional values. This appears to be a characteristic of the postindustrial society. Values change through a process of challenge and accommodation between the system of existing values and the technologies, action pressures, and resultant social changes.

Consistent with these conflicting social influences has been the dual emergence of a social ethic and an individualistic ethic. The individualistic ethic glorifies the freedom of the individual, competition between one person and another, and self-determination as the value goal of life. The social ethic emphasizes the importance of the individual's responsibility to the group and society at large. It assumes that the interactive social system is the primary way of meeting human needs. Golembiewski (1965) says that neither of these ethics by itself is adequate to the task: "Both are morally unspecific; and neither . . . can muster evidence to show it is necessary and sufficient for inducing effective performance under existing conditions" (pp. 45-47).

Three more specific ethical or value systems have been emerging that are relevant for consideration by consultants. These are the scientific ethic, the humanistic ethic, and scientific humanism. Each of these orientations has come increasingly to the fore in the last two decades in response to major social changes. Scientific values tend to emphasize rationality, moderation, flexibility, calculation, planning, and prudence as guidelines. Humanistic values stress freedom, spontaneity, creativity, participation, and self-actualization. Scientific humanism is proposed as an integration of the other two frameworks.

Probably the most important evidences of the application of the scientific ethic are the new science-based analysis and decision-making techniques that are increasingly prevalent in business and government. These techniques, such as operations research and system analysis, call for clarity in the specification of goals and, therefore, serve to make value preferences explicit. As evidence of the humanistic ethic, the humanistic trend in psychology developed by Maslow (1965) is probably most forceful and relevant to the interpersonal aspects of the consulting process. Maslow emphasized openness of communication, mutuality of decision making, personal growth, and fulfillment.

A CODE OF ETHICS

An ethical code for a profession helps to assure fair treatment for clients and provides for the protection of their rights. More explicitly, these are ethical principles for helping behavior:

- Provide professional guidelines, set by historical reference, regarding behavior that is attractive and justifiable to the client;
- Allow professionals to inspire faith in the client that the consultant will behave in a way beneficial to the client;
- Signify that the consultant is committed to do a good job in the client's interest in return for the client's trust and confidence.

In every profession, it has been necessary to establish a code of ethics to protect the interests of clients. This code of ethics represents efforts to reduce to writing some of the more definable rules of conduct. It signifies the voluntary assumption of the obligation of self-discipline above and beyond the requirements of law.

Codes that attempt to deal fully with the ethical dimensions of the professional's role in society can serve a useful function. They are educational, providing members of a profession with guidelines for the kind of ethical behavior that, according to the historic experience of the group, is most likely to justify the confidence of the client. And codes can narrow the area in which the consultant has to struggle with uncertainty.

The Association of Consulting Management Engineers (1966) has outlined the purposes of a code of professional ethics as follows:

- It helps the practitioner determine the propriety of his conduct in his professional relationships;
- It indicates the kind of professional posture that the practitioner must develop and maintain if he is to succeed;
- It gives clients and potential clients a basis for confidence that the professional man sincerely desires to serve them well and places service ahead of financial reward;

- It gives clients a basis for confidence that the professional man will do his work in conformity with professional standards of competence, objectivity, and integrity.

A number of professional organizations have developed codes of ethics for their members. We will briefly examine those of the American Society for Training and Development, the Academy of Management, NTL Institute for Applied Behavioral Science, the American Psychological Association, and the Association of Consulting Management Engineers.

The American Society for Training and Development has published a Code of Ethics (1970). From this code we have chosen the following items as particularly relevant to the best interests of a consultant-client relationship. Consultants shall:

1. Not conduct activities that may cause any colleague or training participant unnecessary embarrassment or disparagement;

2. Not violate confidences or break promises, unless disclosure of confidential information serves professional purposes or is required by law;

3. Limit their activities as facilitators of change to functions for which they have been adequately trained and shall abstain particularly from areas of psychological activity for which they have no professional qualification;

4. Not knowingly distort or misrepresent facts concerning training and development activities to any individual, organization, or employer;

5. Openly share information and data that will advance the state of the professional art;

6. Maintain a professional attitude toward the introduction of new knowledge in the field of training and development;

7. Recognize the desire of individuals and organizations to improve themselves and permit no exploitation of this desire by unethical use of the profession or its members;

8. Recognize that society in general accords status to consultants and in return they have an obligation to serve the needs of society. (p. 30)[4]

The first three rules relate to and uphold the aspect of the profession that encourages the validation of openness and trust between members of the client system and the consultant. Statements four through six concern ethical responsibility, and are designed to protect and support the growth of the profession. Rule seven protects the rights of both clients and the profession. The eighth rule relates to the responsibility

---

[4]Reproduced by special permission from the American Society for Training and Development. Copyright, 1977.

and obligation of the profession toward society in general. The profession should be able to recognize and justify the effect that its practices have on society at large.

The Academy of Management, Division on Organization Development (1976), has adopted a code of ethics, from which we have chosen the following relevant items. Consultants shall:

1. Place the needs of the client organization above their own and not let their own needs interfere in the consulting process;

2. Respect the integrity and protect the welfare and interests of client organizations;

3. Fully inform client organizations of aspects of the potential relationship that might affect the client's decision to enter the relationship;

4. Not misrepresent their own professional qualifications, affiliations, and purposes, or those of the organizations with which they are associated. (pp. 1-2)[5]

The first three rules deal generally with the obligation that any professional should have in dealing with a client and, more specifically, with the OD consulting relationship. The purposes of the fourth rule are to serve the well-being of the client and uphold the profession's good name.

Borrowing from a number of the professional codes of ethics that were mentioned at the beginning of this chapter and from our own experience, we suggest the following code of principles for the professional consultant:

1. *Responsibility*

    The consultant:

    a. Places high value on objectivity and integrity and maintains the highest standards of service;

    b. Plans work in a way that minimizes the possibility that findings will be misleading.

2. *Competence*

    The consultant:

    a. Maintains high standards of professional competence as a responsibility to the public and to the profession;

---

[5] From Academy of Management, "Proposed Code of Ethics," in *Organization Development Division Newsletter*, 1976, Winter, pp. 1-2. Reprinted with permission of the publisher.

b. Recognizes the boundaries of his or her competence and does not offer services that fail to meet professional standards;

c. Assists clients in obtaining professional help for aspects of the project that fall outside the boundaries of his or her own competence;

d. Refrains from undertaking any activity in which his or her personal problems are likely to result in inferior professional service or harm to the client.

3. *Moral and Legal Standards*

The consultant shows sensible regard for the social codes and moral expectations of the community in which he or she works.

4. *Misrepresentation*

The consultant avoids misrepresentation of his or her own professional qualifications, affiliations, and purposes and those of the organization with which he or she is associated.

5. *Confidentiality*

The consultant:

a. Reveals information received in confidence only to the appropriate authorities;

b. Maintains confidentiality of professional communications about individuals;

c. Informs client of the limits of confidentiality;

d. Maintains confidentiality in preservation and disposition of records.

6. *Client Welfare*

The consultant:

a. Defines the nature of his or her loyalties and responsibilities in possible conflicts of interest, such as between the client and the employer of the consultant, and keeps all concerned parties informed of these commitments;

b. Attempts to terminate a consulting relationship when it is reasonably clear that the client is not benefiting from it;

c. Continues being responsible for the welfare of the client, in cases involving referral, until the responsibility is assumed by the professional to whom the client is referred or until the relationship with the client has been terminated by mutual agreement.

7. *Announcement of Services*

The consultant adheres to professional standards rather than solely economic rewards in making known his or her availability for professional services.

8. *Interprofessional Relations*

The consultant acts with integrity toward colleagues in consultation and in other professions.

9. *Remuneration*

The consultant ensures that the financial arrangements for his or her professional services are in accordance with professional standards that safeguard the best interests of the client and the profession.

10. *Responsibility Toward Organization*

The consultant respects the rights and reputation of the organization with which he or she is associated.

11. *Promotional Activities*

The consultant, when associated with the development or promotion of products offered for commercial sale, will ensure that the products are presented in a factual way.

Nevertheless, the adoption of a code, no matter how complete and detailed, is not enough. Members of the profession should study the code, know the reasons for its provisions, and understand its general importance as a part of professional competence.

Simply establishing a code of ethics does not guarantee a change in the ways that consultants function. Regardless of how good a code of professional ethics may be, it will be ineffective unless there is some practical system of enforcement that is accepted by practicing professionals. A lack of penalties is the most basic reason why even well-constructed codes have not had significant impact on consulting practice. Although a number of professional associations have developed well-defined procedures for handling alleged violations of their codes, some of the most clear-cut sanctions have been developed and publicized by the Association of Consulting Management Engineers, Inc., and the American Psychological Association, Inc. (APA).

The APA developed a code in 1953 to guide the psychological profession in the earlier stages of its development. After its experience in applying the code, the APA revised it in 1959, 1963, and, again, in 1966.

The Committee on Scientific and Professional Ethics (CSPEC) was established as an instrument by which members of the APA could judge their peers concerning alleged violations of the code. While many potential infractions of the APA code of ethics have been called to the attention of the CSPEC, the committee has not found it necessary to confront the alleged offender in every instance. Sometimes the documentation provided by complainants is inadequate, or the behavior described as unethical is not necessarily so. Many situations are solved constructively by correspondence about the circumstances surrounding the behavior or activities in question.

The APA and its members are concerned with the professional conduct of persons who purport to be psychologists but do not belong to the association. In the case of nonmembers, however, disciplinary action can be taken only by the government or other agencies that have jurisdiction over the person. The CSPEC (1968) deals only with questions of ethics, and then only in an investigatory and advisory role. Disciplinary action is the responsibility of the board of directors of the APA, which takes into account the findings of the committee.

The APA has used the findings rendered by CSPEC as an index of the serviceability and fairness of its code. It has also compiled a casebook containing disguised material drawn from the findings of the committee, and cited the principles involved and the conclusions reached. The *Casebook on Ethical Standards of Psychologists* (1967) furnishes precedents for the APA and for local ethics committees, and it is also used for educative purposes by psychologists in general.

For the APA, the code has both a judicial and an educative function. It represents the set of standards from which decisions are made, and it also constitutes a guide to ethical practices. Taken together, the casebook and the code are designed to clarify the judicial functions and to serve an educative purpose at the same time.

The teeth in the judicial role of such a self-policing committee is that members who are found guilty of unethical behavior, as measured against the code, are expelled from the association or placed on probation.

One other development in the enforcement of ethical behavior is the requirement in some states that consultants be licensed, a requirement already in effect for many psychologists. Flagrant violations of the accepted code, as judged by the association judicial committee, should result in the debarring of the consultant. Such potent sanctions would surely enforce the code as the accepted law of professional behavior.

Codes usually are addressed to the correction of known deficiencies and malpractices experienced in the past. However, codes falter in dealing with the unforeseeable or dimly envisioned future. They become a minimal expectation for improving the past and can only suggest a principle of decision making for the future. When novel, complicated, or previously unrecorded situations occur, the consultant must stand alone in his decision making (Beck, 1971).

The most important aspect of formulating a code is the acceptance of a basic norm of morality that will properly sustain the code and indicate practical applications to consultants in situations too specific to be covered by the code. The effectiveness of this depends on the competence of the consultant.

Many groups besides the specialists' professional societies are defining and using competency-based criteria for membership. Such groups include the Institute of Management Consultants, the International Association of Applied Social Scientists, NTL Institute for Applied Behavioral Science, Association for Creative Change, Society of Professional Management Consultants, Organization Renewal, Inc., and the International Consultants Foundation.

ILLUSTRATIVE ETHICAL DILEMMAS IN CONSULTING

There are some ethical dilemmas in consulting that we see as present or potential challenges in the consulting process. Although both the consultant and the client bring into the consulting process their normative expectations of the relationship, these expectations are not always in agreement. Three of these are as follows:

1. The clients' expectations of the nature of the help they need and how they should get it;
2. The intrusion of ethical standards acquired by the consultant in his other professional experiences; and
3. The conflicts between ethics identified with the consultant's nonprofessional life and value judgments that are peculiar to a consultation process.

A brief discussion of each of these dilemmas follows.

The integrity of the consultant can be challenged when demands from the client push the limits of the consultant's ethical concepts and guidelines. The manner in which such a problem is handled is both a technical and an ethical consideration for the consultant. The client may want a particular answer or method that the consultant, for technical professional reasons, refrains from offering. Such technical, professional, and ethical judgment and assessment requires the ultimate in flexibility on the part of the consultant in order to accomplish an effective relationship and to achieve the client's goals. There must be a mutual accommodation between the expectations of the client and the consultant.

Consultants often function as social scientists, engineers, or educators, as well as professional consultants. This overlap in roles makes complete role segregation difficult, and ethical problems arise in the consultant's attempts to integrate these professional affiliations and orientations. The consultant may find that the norms introduced from professional associations are threatened by the demands of client behavior and the here-and-now consulting situation. Consequently, a conflict develops between the ethical demands of the two roles.

Because they are less systematically articulated by the consultant, nonprofessional aspects of the consultant's values present a less definable ethical problem. However, the norms of the consultant's nonprofessional life do present dilemmas in certain client situations. For example, there is the question of whether a consultant can ethically engage with a client system whose purpose and goals are opposed to his own personal, religious, or political doctrine. Should a consultant who is a conscientious objector to the use of military force to settle international problems allow himself to become engaged in consultation for a national defense project? Should a consultant who favors strict gun control consult with the National Rifle Association?

The examples described would be ethical only if the consultant's relationship with the client system were completely divorced from the consultant's personal doctrine and the client was made aware of the consultant's values. These circumstances are not likely, and a consultant would be justified in declining such an assignment because of a conflict of personal norms. This is an ethical problem because its solution involves the future of the consultant's personal doctrine and nonprofessional associations, as well as the effectiveness and integrity of the consultation process in which the consultant is about to engage.

The consultant must personally resolve these ethical conflicts. In such situations, we have found it helpful to seek guidance from respected associates who could offer constructive advice based on their experience and insights.

These potential dilemmas should receive attention in the preservice and inservice training of consultants. There should be opportunities for training in making choices, not toward standard solutions, but toward solutions that are right for the individual consultant and for the client.

The Manipulation Dilemma

The recognition that consulting usually involves, directly or indirectly, the deliberate influencing of human attitudes, values, and behavior creates a variety of ethical ambiguities. The product of the consultant's work may meet the immediate needs of the client, yet its long-range consequences and its effect on other units of the client system may be problematic. It is necessary, therefore, that the consultant be concerned with the larger impact of the processes and outcome to which he or she contributes. But how do consultants cope with the role of influencing others' personal and social destinies? One solution lies in the "voluntary nature of the change relationship" (Lippitt, 1958), with the consultant impressing this fact on the client and ensuring that the client understands and accepts it.

Kelman (1969) discusses in depth this same ethical dilemma for the social scientist/consultant, whose work has a manipulative nature. The basic dilemma has two dimensions. In the eyes of those persons who hold the enhancement of man's freedom of choice as a fundamental value, any deliberate influencing of the behavior of others constitutes a violation of their basic humanity. On the other hand, effective behavior change involves some degree of utilization of power and control, and a potential imposition of the change agent's values on the client system. According to Kelman:

> The two horns of the dilemma, then, are represented by the view that any manipulation of human behavior inherently violates a fundamental value, but that there exists no formula for so structuring an effective change situation that such manipulation is totally absent. (p. 33)[6]

Kelman cites two dangers that consultants face in influencing the client toward change:

> One is the failure to recognize that [the consultant] is engaged in the control of the client's behavior. The other is intoxication with the goodness of what he is doing for and to the client, which in turn leads to a failure to recognize the ambiguity of the control that he exercises. (p. 37)[7]

The consultant must recognize these dangers in order to take steps to control them.

Kelman suggests three broad, generalized steps that are designed to mitigate the manipulative aspect of behavior change efforts, and he adds appropriate actions applied to the field of the practitioner, the

---

[6]From Herbert C. Kelman, "Manipulation of Human Behavior: An Ethical Dilemma for the Social Scientist," in the *Journal of Social Issues*, 1965, *21*(2), pp. 31-46. Reprinted by permission.

[7]See Footnote 6.

applied researcher, and the basic researcher. These helpful guides to the professionally competent consultant are as follows:

1. Increasing one's own and others' active awareness of the manipulative aspects of one's work and the ethical ambiguities inherent therein, by labeling one's own values to oneself and client and by allowing the client to talk back;

2. Deliberately building protection against or resistance to manipulation into the process, by minimizing one's own values and by maximizing the client's values as the dominant criteria for change;

3. Setting the enhancement of freedom of choice as a central positive goal for one's practice, by using professional skills and relationships to increase the client's ability to choose and range of choices.

Benne (1959) refers to two ethical dilemmas that are relevant to the consultant's role. The first of these dilemmas deals with internal conflicts arising between the different interests of the consultant's "scientist self" and "consultant self" in dealing with the client. As Benne says, the conflict may take the form "of anxiety that one is losing his scientific hard-headedness in enjoying the psychic rewards of helping one's client" (p. 64). Benne suggests that the consultant's personal dilemmas, anxieties, and uneasiness may be reduced if the person gives time and thought to the articulation and formulation of his or her own civic, religious, and personal philosophies and moralities—a precondition for adequately recognizing and handling ethical issues that arise in the consulting relationship.

This ethical dilemma is similar to the one discussed earlier that arises in the selection of clients by the consultant. Different criteria may include the needs of the client system, the needs of the consultant, potential learning for the consultant, the consultant's personal attraction to a client, and the potential contribution made to society by dealing with a particular client.

ETHICAL DILEMMAS OF INTERNAL OR EXTERNAL CONSULTANTS

One might assume that there would be some differences in the guidelines for the ethical behavior of an internal consultant and an external consultant. The major difference can be attributed to the objectivity, or lack of it, with which a consultant might behave because of the positional difference.

Collier (1962) says that the way you look at a business depends on where you happen to be. It makes a big difference whether you are on the outside looking in or on the inside looking out. If you are a member of an organization, you can never quite see the organization in the same way as those who are not members. As a member you have certain responsibilities, certain loyalties, certain hopes and fears that inevitably color and enrich your perceptions of the organization. Your frame of reference is significantly different from the frame of reference of the outsider looking in.

In 1969, the American Management Association conducted a twenty-month study of the internal consultant process as used by approximately sixty commercial firms (Dekom, 1969). The results of their findings were reported functionally as follows:

The Consulting Staffs were generally:

- Well educated, analytical, perceptive, diplomatic, broadly experienced, and temperamentally suited to a staff role;
- Depleted through promotions of good people to operating positions;
- Held to high personal and professional standards of conduct.

Staff Training and Development:

- Objective training was received outside the company;
- Staff was furnished with a handbook of professional behavior.

Compensation:

- Was not dependent on the success of the individual consulting project.

Source of Assignment:

- Most assignments originated with requests from a client-subsidiary or a subordinate-level manager.

Launching Assignment:

- Assignment was launched by a letter providing an overview of the scope of the work.
- Project objective outlined by client;
- Probable involvement of client personnel spelled out by consultant;
- Estimate of on-the-job and elapsed times done by consultant;
- Estimate of fees and out-of-pocket expenses done by consultant.

Reports:

- Both oral and written reports made to client;
- Client reviewed report draft before finalization;
- Significant client objections to report accommodated in final report;
- Most consultants reported only to client;
- Reports included plan of action to follow;
- Relations with client treated as confidential;
- Findings and recommendations not reported to higher management without the client's permission.

Implementation:

- Consultant assisted in implementation;
- Effectiveness of consultation measured by actions taken by client and by repeat requests for help.

Fees:

- Cases in which consultants charged clients directly were more effective than those in which the cost was charged to a firm's overhead.

Use of Public Consultants:

- Internal consultants advised on the use of outside help when there was a peak demand for trained personnel, unusual expertise was needed, or the appearance and the fact of complete objectivity were necessary.

From the experience of the firms contacted in this research, it can be concluded that, except for the reduced objectivity with which the internal consultant is handicapped, there was little difference in the relevance of ethical guidelines for the internal consultant and for external consultants. The same code of ethics could apply. From our discussions with both internal and external helpers, we feel that the ethical standards and concern in consultation are relevant to one and all.

SUMMARY

All ethics can be called personal statements—values accepted by individuals in the profession and adhered to during their individual consultations. Many of these are agreed on en masse by the members of the profession, as are most of the ethics presented earlier in this chapter.

But some ethics are very personal and are established by each individual to mesh with his or her consulting style. These should not be in conflict with the established ethics of the profession; instead, they should expand and define more clearly the individual's own basic motivations and style.

As we have previously observed (Lippitt, 1969):

> Both research and practical experience underscore the fact that the single most important factor in the practice of ethical behavior is the individual's personal code and standards. Each person represents in his own life the influence of his environment and his experience, and this contributes to the criteria he uses to appraise the ethical implications of particular situations. (pp. 10-12)[8]

We have suggested practical guides to evaluate the proper decision in a particular situation (Lippitt, 1969, pp. 10-12).

Even as the consultant's career begins, he or she must develop a personal code of ethics. This requires soul searching and conscious awareness of the realm of the profession in which one is dealing. Naïvete can be no excuse for a lack of ethical standards or for practicing ethics that are unreliable or harmful to the consulting relationship.

On the other hand, consultants should be urged to move out of the ethics gulch and to avoid the practice of "ethiscuity" (Bancroft, 1971), which is defined as the promiscuous taking of refuge in ethics in order to protect oneself from potentially threatening and anxiety-producing relationships with clients, thereby refusing service to them.

The process of continually evaluating one's code of ethics and the application of those ethics must continue throughout one's professional life, with the use of trusted colleagues as testers and clarifiers. The acquisition of ethical competence reduces anxiety and increases effectiveness in the situational decision making that is a constant in the consulting process.

---

[8]From Gordon Lippitt, *Organization Renewal*. Englewood Cliffs, NJ: Prentice-Hall, 1969, pp. 10-12. Reprinted by permission of the publisher.

Chapter 6
Action Research and Evaluation in the Consulting Process

The collection of data is basic to practically all consulting situations. In defining goals and diagnosing causes, both the client and the consultant collect and analyze needed data. As Weisbord (1976) states:

> Collecting data on which to base a diagnosis can be as simple as brainstorming or as complex as a "grand design" research methodology involving hypotheses, instruments, and computer analysis. Complexity aside, there are four ways to collect data:
>
> 1. *Observation.* Watch what people do in meetings, on the job, on the phone, etc.
>
> 2. *Reading.* Follow the written record—speeches, reports, charts, graphs, etc.
>
> 3. *Interviews.* Question everyone involved with a particular project.
>
> 4. *Survey.* Use standard questionnaires or design your own. Surveys are most useful when they ask for information not readily obtainable in any other way, such as attitudes, perceptions, opinions, preferences, beliefs, etc.
>
> All four methods of data collection can be used to isolate the two major kinds of discrepancy—between what people say (formal) and what they do (informal), and between what is (organization as it exists) and what ought to be (appropriate environmental fit). The trick is not to use any particular methods, but to sort the evidence of one's senses into some categories that encourage sensible decisions. (p. 435)[1]

The authors wish to acknowledge the help of Mary Roberts in the literature search for this chapter.

[1]From M. R. Weisbord, "Organizational Diagnosis: Six Places to Look for Trouble with or Without a Theory." In *Group & Organization Studies: The International Journal for Group Facilitators*, 1976, *1*(4), pp. 430-447. Reprinted by permission of the publisher.

We think the appropriate use of tests should be added to Weisbord's list.

In this chapter, we examine three aspects of data collection/research in relationship to consultation:

1. Some general definitions and guidelines to data collections;
2. The need for evaluating the consulting process;
3. Action research as an integral part of most consulting situations.

DATA COLLECTION: AN OVERVIEW

Most clients who are served by consultants function largely through groups or organizations. These client systems must plan, organize, execute, and test—and testing is fact finding. Research is a phase of fact finding that is not the by-product of regular operating procedure and reporting. Research usually starts with some hypothesis to be tested.

Some research methods are more applicable to consulting situations than others. The choice of method depends on the nature of the inquiry and on how much control of the experimental variables is desired. The following methods are not mutually exclusive:

1. *Laboratory Experiment:* controlled manipulations of certain variables at the possible expense of typicality;
2. *Field Experiment:* partially controlled manipulation of conditions in an actual field setting; more applicable to reality and more expensive;
3. *Field Studies:* no manipulation, but exhaustive observation of a limited situation; gives an ongoing picture, which is difficult to generalize;
4. *Survey:* observations taken from a large cross section of a population by one of many sampling techniques; relatively inexpensive, but gives only a cross-sectional or static picture;
5. *Action Research:* designed to yield practical results on a problem of operation; involves subjects or clients in data processing;
6. *Research in Existing Written Sources:* easily available and inexpensive, but not always applicable, and open to questions of accuracy.

When preparing for data collection, the client and consultant must formulate the necessary questions in research terms (not as a value belief question, using terms such as "should" or "ought to"). And they must reduce the operation's scope to a practical cost in time and money. The data required must be defined, and the possibility of translating findings into action must be pre-established.

Advantages and Disadvantages of Data-Collection Methods

LABORATORY EXPERIMENT

As Festinger (1953) states:

> A laboratory experiment may be defined as one in which the investigator creates a situation with the exact conditions he wants to have and in which he controls some, and manipulates other, variables. (p. 137)[2]

This method is especially suited for a situation in which precise control of the variable(s) is desired and possible.

Some advantages of the laboratory-experiment approach to research is that it offers:

- More control of variable(s);
- Better observation;
- Less expensive operation;
- Easier administration.

Some disadvantages of the laboratory-experiment approach in data collection are:

- The question of how typical the results are; do they represent reality?
- The results are difficult to generalize;
- Some criteria cannot be taken into the laboratory as variables.

FIELD EXPERIMENTS

Kurt Lewin (1945) observed that:

> Although it appears to be possible to study certain problems of society in experimentally created, smaller laboratory groups, we shall also have to develop research techniques that will permit us to do real experiments within existing "natural" social groups. In my opinion, the practical and theoretical importance of these types is of the first magnitude. (p. 9)[3]

The setting for a field experiment is some existing social situation; it is real. The experimenter manipulates conditions in field experiments in order to determine causal relations.

---

[2] From Leon Festinger, *Research Methods in the Behavioral Sciences*. Hinsdale, Il: Dryden Press, 1953, p. 137. Reprinted with permission of the publisher.

[3] Reprinted from Kurt Lewin, "Research Center for Group Dynamics," *Sociometry*, 1945, 8, p. 9. Used with permission of the publisher.

Naturally, an advantage of field experiments is that they are more applicable to reality.

Disadvantages of field experiments include:

- The variables are more difficult to control;
- They are more expensive;
- It is necessary to get operations support;
- Ethical questions.

FIELD STUDIES

The field-study method provides a thorough account of the process under investigation. Field investigators study a single community or a single group in terms of its social structure. They attempt to measure and observe the ongoing processes, recording the social interactions that reflect the positions and attitudes of people.

Some advantages of collecting data with the field-study method are:

- It gives an overall picture;
- "Living in"—getting a more accurate feel for the natural environment or situation.

Disadvantages of field studies include the following:

- The data are difficult to quantify;
- There is a danger of subjectivity on the part of the investigator;
- It is difficult to verify the data with other researchers;
- Replicating the experiment is difficult.

SURVEY

The survey method of research depends on data collected directly from a particular representative sample of people. It is a tool for both basic and applied research and is frequently used in the consulting situation.

Some advantages of the survey-research method are that it:

- Measures directly the population being studied;
- Is relatively inexpensive;
- Is easy to quantify;
- Uses well-worked-out procedures.

Some disadvantages of the survey-research method are that it:

- Is applicable to only a point in time;
- Is essentially static and similar to a snapshot;
- Produces data difficult to interpret for action;
- Requires an appropriate sample that is difficult to select.

ACTION RESEARCH

The action-research method is usually used to solve a problem in operation. It involves the client in data collection relevant to the consultation process, such as diagnosing a problem and evaluating the effects of action.

Some advantages of action research are as follows:

- People tend to utilize the findings;
- People are likely to become involved in the process;
- There is economy in the collecting of data.

Disadvantages of the action-research method include:

- The necessity of training fact finders;
- The necessity of obtaining the support of people in the operation;
- The subjectivity resulting from direct involvement;
- The researcher must relinquish some decision-making power.

RESEARCH IN EXISTING WRITTEN SOURCES

A consultant and client often can find data from existing documents and letters, life histories, accounts of small-group process, annual reports, diagrams, and other sources.

Doing research in existing written sources has the following advantages:

- The sources are easily available;
- The research is inexpensive.

Disadvantages of this research method include:

- It is not always applicable;
- The researcher may not be sure of some of the data;
- The data are difficult to synthesize;
- The data are selective

The Use of Interviewing

No matter which research methods are chosen by the consultant, interviewing is a basic tool common to all except the research of written sources. All consultants use the interview as a data-collection process sometime during the helping process. Such interviews might be with an individual or a group. The group interview can trigger more ideas, open up communications, and start appropriate action.

The results of an interview are always the joint product of the interviewer and the respondent in the interaction. Respondents usually will communicate only when they feel it is to their advantage. The possibility of being able to check up on facts produces some extrinsic or negative motivation. There is intrinsic motivation in the satisfaction most respondents feel in having an opportunity to converse with an empathic listener. The interviewer thinks about what the other person is saying and why, rather than planning how he will phrase the forthcoming questions. At the same time, the interviewer has to direct the conversation so that its content will meet the objectives of the interview. The wording of questions must bridge the respondent's language framework and the interviewer's objectives. The respondent's frame of reference (personal experience) for using words can be revealed by the reasons he gives for his answers.

Whether data collection is conducted by the consultant or is done by the client with the consultants serving as technical advisers, the client has an important role to play in developing acceptance of the research, enlisting support of the respondents, and stimulating confidence in the research.

When deciding between the use of consultant-executed data or action research, one should consider which method does the following:

- Establishes greater objectivity?
- Has a better focus on fundamental problems?
- Secures the required knowledge of the problem?
- Provides better cooperation and better utilization of findings?
- Is better at adapting the skills and resources that are available?
- Offers the better choice of financial by-products—cash outlay, diverted cost of staff time, staff skill gained?

Choosing a Data-Collection Method

Whether a certain method of collecting data would be relevant to a particular consulting situation depends on how a number of factors are perceived by the client and the consultant. The following questions offer some criteria for determining whether a particular consultation lends itself to evaluation and/or to research.

1. How complex is the consulting problem? If the problem is really a number of problems or is very complex, it may not be possible to apply research methods to the process.

2. How much time will be required to get the information? If a consultation covers a span of years, it may not be possible to do research evaluation, although longitudinal studies are needed.

3. Is the question one of the values of operations? If the question is a matter of policy, rather than of measurable operations, it may arouse doubts of whether data collection is feasible.

4. What will be the cost of securing the facts? If the financial demand of such research is too great, it might make data collection impractical.

5. What will be the nonfinancial demands on the consultant and client? Any consulting relationship should assess such matters as the need for support, time, public relations, and stress tolerance in determining the possibility of doing data collection/ evaluation.

6. Is it feasible that the consultation process will be helped through the obtaining of evidence? If the data are difficult or impossible to obtain, it might be questionable whether valuation will be possible.

7. Is starting some action the best way to collect the needed data?

EVALUATING THE CONSULTING PROCESS

Those who teach and practice professional consultation have expressed some concern about the dearth of published research evaluating the consulting process. Only a limited amount of research on consultation has been conducted or published, which is in sharp contrast to the extensive amount of consultation that has been done by private consultants, academic personnel, and internal consultants in organizations. Virtually every kind of business, government, and service organization has been involved in consultation to some extent. Judgments of the success of such consultation usually have been based on expressions of faith in the general value of consulting, but consultation has received little critical evaluation based on research findings.

Our experience has indicated that evaluative research is needed by both the consultant and the client. Our first research study not only resulted in a publication (Lippitt, 1959), but also was invaluable as action research on the client's problem.

The general literature on consulting has grown along with the professional practice. An extensive annotated bibliography on consultation was compiled by Hollander and published in 1972 by the Bureau of Business and Economic Research, Graduate School of Business Administration, Michigan State University. The number of entries increased from 478 entries in the 1962 edition to almost twice that number in the 1972 edition. However, about 85 percent of the entries were descriptive, theoretical, or case reports. Most of the research

---

Gordon Lippitt presented a portion of this section as a paper entitled "Research on the Consulting Process" at the annual conference of the Academy of Management, Orlando, Florida, August 1977.

studies reported were done by private consulting firms and public agencies.

In a survey of consultants and clients (Bidwell & Lippitt, 1971) done at George Washington University, we found some key obstacles to research on the consulting process (see Table 1). According to the seventy-five persons who were surveyed, the key obstacles were lack of time, inadequate frame of reference for evaluations, and inability to develop measurable objectives of the consultation. Although it is understandable that lack of time and money is important, it is interesting to note the number of respondents who indicated their inability to establish a frame of reference for conducting such research.

Table 1.
Obstacles to Consulting Research

OBSTACLES	NUMBER OF RESPONSES [a] (N-52)
1. Lack of time	20
2. Lack of a frame of reference	15
3. Failure of consultant and client to determine client expectations in measurable terms	14
4. Lack of money for research	12
5. Need to convince management	9
6. Lack of effective research methods and tools	6
7. Need for adequate facilities and resources	3
8. Lack of cooperation between client and consultant	2
9. Magnitude of the research	2

[a]Twenty-three respondents did not answer all the questions and sixteen gave two or more responses.

In a recent publication (Swartz & Lippitt, 1975), a conceptual model was presented for evaluating the consultative situation, as shown in Figure 4.

The following are some brief explanations and definitions of the four interdependent elements that are diagramed in Figure 4.

Research and Evaluation Areas

Client/Consultant Relationship. This area relates to the evaluation of the personal and professional relationships between client, client system, and consultant. These relationships often have a major impact on the final outcome of the consulting process.

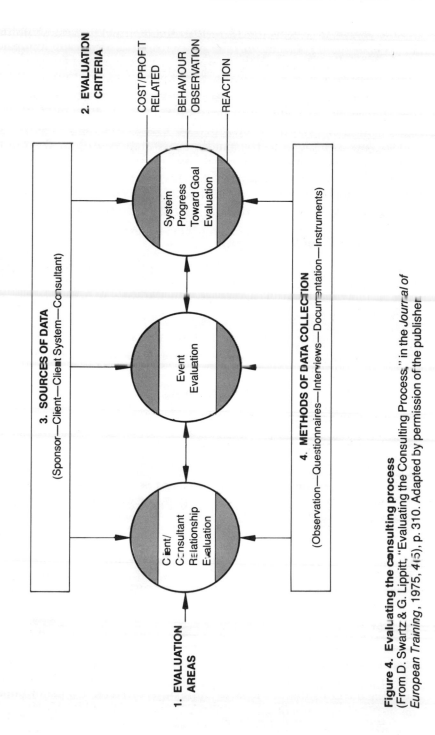

Figure 4.   Evaluating the consulting process
(From D. Swartz & G. Lippitt, "Evaluating the Consulting Process," in the *Journal of European Training*, 1975, 4(5), p. 310. Adapted by permission of the publisher)

Evaluation of Consulting/Training Events. This evaluation area covers significant consulting interventions, such as survey-feedback meetings, skill training, conflict-resolution meetings, and other important, milestone activities. Assessing the impact and contribution of each of these types of event on the overall project can provide important information, both for designing future projects with the client and for improving similar events that will take place in the current project.

Progress Toward Specific Goals. This area relates to the client system's progress toward achievement of prestated goals and the contribution made by the consultation toward this progress. Evaluation of overall results helps to answer the client's question, "Was the money I invested in consultation returned, at least, by the results achieved?"

Research and Evaluation Criteria

Cost/Profit Related. Some "hard-measure" criteria are developed to determine as directly as possible the effect of consultation on the achievement of specified results. Some examples of specified results related to cost/profit are:

- Consulting time and expense (estimate vs. actual);
- Consulting-event outcomes that result in increased sales, decreased costs;
- Trend changes in safety record, grievances, turnover, absenteeism, theft.

Within the cost-related evaluation criteria there are three approaches to measurement that can be considered:

- Specific goal attainment by a specified time;
- Trend tracking vs. a plan or estimated performance;
- Spot checks of performance vs. hoped-for change, e.g., a downward trend has been reversed.

Behavior Observation. These criteria call for documentation of significant changes observed in individual, group, or organizational behavior that resulted directly from the consulting process or from an event influenced by the consulting process. Some examples of observed behavior change are:

- The client is much more relaxed and is functioning in a more assertive manner;
- A change has occurred in the organization structure, simplifying lines of communications;
- Event participants demonstrate that they can plan for and conduct problem-solving meetings.

Reaction. These criteria relate to the reactions of the client and the client system to the consulting process. They report feelings, attitudes, and points of view as these change over time. Some examples of reaction criteria measurements are:

- The client's expressed feelings about the consulting relationship;
- The participants' evaluation of a training event;
- The reactions of the client system as expressed through a series of attitude surveys during the course of the consulting process.

Sources of Data

There are four sources of data for an evaluation system. Each of them is defined as follows:

The Sponsor is a person (or persons) who can significantly influence the consulting process and who has a strong interest in the initiation, progress, and final outcome of the consulting process. In some instances the sponsor is the client's supervisor. Many times (particularly when working at the top of the organization), the sponsor is the client, e.g., the president. The sponsor also could be a group of people such as a city council, advisory board, executive committee, or board of directors.

The Client is the person who makes the "go or no go" decision about events and directions within the sphere of the project.

The Client System is any person or group directly involved in, or affected by, the consulting project.

The Consultant is the helper (or helpers) whose expertise has been contracted for by the client. The helper may be internal to the client system or external to it. There may also be a combination of internal and external helpers.

Methods of Data Collection

Data can be collected in a wide variety of ways. The following are five methods that are most frequently used to collect data for evaluation of the consulting process.

Observation. Individual and group behavior is observed and recorded as it relates to the job to be done. Also observed and recorded are the ways in which systems are functioning, e.g., flow charting, decision trees, PERT charting.

Questionnaires. Formats are specially designed or standardized, asking for individual written responses concerning attitude, viewpoints, opinions, and perceptions.

Interviews. Individuals or groups are interviewed face-to-face or by telephone to gain their in-depth perceptions, specific examples, ideas, and feelings.

Documentation. Archival records, current records, and specially-recorded data are used to show trends and changes resulting from the consulting process.

Instruments. Devices are specially designed for data collection with the purpose of stimulating individual feedback about a situation and to provide a framework for evaluation discussions between client, client systems, and consultant.

It is interesting to note in Table 2 that, although a number of additional data-collection methods were listed in the Bidwell and Lippitt survey, questionnaires were most frequently cited.

Table 2.
Methods Used for the Evaluation of Consultation

METHODS	NUMBER OF RESPONSES [a] (N-64)
1. Questionnaires	32
2. Interviews	16
3. Client reports	14
4. Efficiency reports	10
5. Discussions with client	9
6. Periodic testing	9
7. Inspections and visits	8
8. Consultant's ratings	8
9. Postevaluation immediately after consultation	7
10. Surveys of reactions to consultation	7
11. Surveys and operations audit	4
12. Follow-up testing (6 months to 1 year later)	1

[a]Eleven respondents did not list any methods, and thirteen listed four different methods.

At this point, it should be reiterated that every consulting situation is a data-collection process. In fact, the Bidwell and Lippitt survey showed that action research was the most frequently mentioned purpose for data collection in the consulting relationship (see Table 3). However, there is some difficulty in attempting to look at action research as simply a research method or a technology of consultation, because the total consultation process is essentially a program of action research.

Table 3.
Purposes for the Evaluation of Consultation

PURPOSES	NUMBER OF RESPONSES [a] (N-75)
1. Action research on the problem	68
2. Evaluating the consulting process	55
3. Satisfaction of client	53
4. Improved skill or performance of consultant	38
5. Other [b]	23

[a] Fifty-four respondents indicated three or more purposes for evaluating consultation, and fourteen listed five purposes.

[b] The category *Other* included such purposes as increased business income, change in organization relationships, value to organization, results in productivity and profits, program results, relationship to mission objectives, and supervisor's appraisal of value of consultation.

ACTION RESEARCH: THE CONSULTING PROCESS AT WORK

If action research is considered as a process—a continuous series of occurrences—it may be defined as

The process of systematically collecting research data about an ongoing system relative to some objective, goal, or need of that system; feeding these data back into the system; taking actions by altering selected variables within the system based both on the data and on hypotheses; and evaluating the results of actions by collecting more data. (French & Bell, 1973, pp. 84-85)[4]

---

[4] From Wendell L. French and Cecil H. Bell, Jr., *Organizational Development: Behavioral Science Interventions for Organization Improvement*, © 1973, pp. 84-85, 86. By permission of Prentice-Hall, Inc., Englewood Cliffs, New Jersey.

One of the important concepts involved in action research is that "The roles of researcher and subject may change and reverse, the subjects becoming researchers and the researchers engaging in action steps" (Lippitt, 1973, p. 55).

The model illustrated in Figure 5 shows a process that could either involve an outside consultant or rely on individuals within the organization. The model also allows for the important point that action research is "Sometimes treating the same problem through several cycles and sometimes moving to different problems in each cycle" (French & Bell, 1973, p. 86).

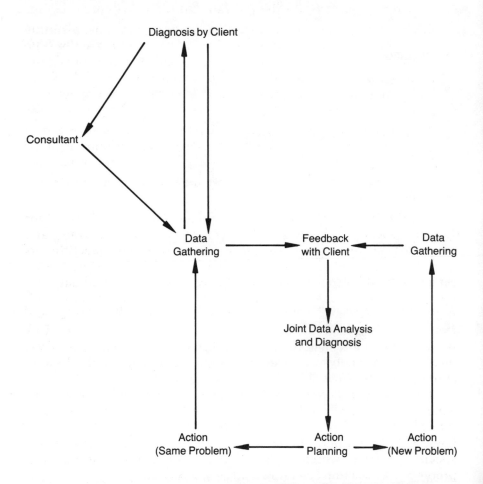

Figure 5. Model of action research in consultation (Courtesy of Mary Roberts.)

When looking at action research as a process, we should include at least four major steps (Roberts, 1975):

1. Data collection may: be preceded by a tentative diagnosis of a particular problem area (or may not be); utilize numerous instruments available for collecting data on task, environmental, or attitude climate; involve the training of clients in data-collection skills and procedures.

2. Feedback of data to client should be: within a short period of time; worthwhile to the participants; specific enough to aid analysis and discussion; without value judgments; given in an open, supportive climate; relevant to desired goals of the client.

3. Action planning should: include in some aspect of the planning all the people who will be involved in the resulting actions; be relevant to the client's goals; be a close collaboration among the consultants, administrators, and participants involved; be feasible within the systems framework; be based on implications drawn from data collected.

4. Action should: have built-in standards by which to measure progress and results; lead to further data collection and change, if evaluation shows it to be going in the wrong direction relative to the chosen goals, be continuously based on research, once the process has begun.

The use of action research began in the field of social science. Kurt Lewin, a social psychologist, is recognized as a major innovator and advocate of action research. He became aware that active practitioners were tackling problems without first having standards for measuring progress. He was concerned over efforts being expended without gaining the learning that results from knowing whether the action is heading in the right direction. Lewin felt that research (i.e., fact finding and evaluation) could fill this gap and that action research was the link between the practitioners and the experimenters. Again the stress was on collaboration between the people of science and the people of action (French & Bell, 1973).

Action research lends itself to a diversity of goals, and the variations among practitioners are numerous. Lewin separated action research into the following two broad categories: (1) investigation of general laws, which contributes to theory and practice; and (2) diagnosis of a specific situation, which leads to the solution of pressing, practical problems. A consultant should be interested in both.

Jenks (1972) broke down action research into four categories: (1) diagnostic (a researcher diagnoses and makes recommendations, which may or may not be put into effect); (2) participant; (3) empirical (requiring extensive records and posing several limitations); and (4) experimental. The experimental goal for action research is recognized as the most difficult but, like Lewin's investigation of general laws, it contributes to scientific knowledge and provides models of action research. The client's goal in action research is the one being emphasized in this chapter.

The basic four-step process described in this chapter may be altered or expanded to meet specific consulting situations or projects. One weakness that may be ascribed to action research is that there is not a single and exclusive way to carry it out. On the other hand, this can also be considered a strength, especially in consultations. The variety of projects and areas in which action research has been utilized literally demands the flexibility that both the model and the process offer.

As with many other consulting technologies, action research may seem to be just common sense, to use parts of other technologies as its own, or to be but a part of another process. None of these can be considered weaknesses in the literal sense; if anything, they each add strength to the integrative functioning of the consulting process. Perhaps the difficulty in looking at action research as a separate consulting technology has been its similarity to the essence of consulting itself.

To encourage research in and about consultation, we suggest that the consultant take the following action steps to cope with existing blocks to research and evaluation:

1. Change the attitudes of clients toward the need for research;
2. Give research in consultation the status it requires;
3. Encourage clients to secure the financial backing required by data collection;
4. Generate between client and consultant the cooperation and coordination that is required for research;
5. Educate and train students and consultants to appreciate the importance of research;
6. Train students and consultants in the tools and methods of research.

There is no single right way to evaluate or do research in consultation. Consultants and clients should create evaluation and research methods appropriate to their needs and based on proven principles of scientific inquiry. This is essential to the problem-solving process that constitutes consultation.

Chapter 7
The Consultant's Skills, Competencies, and Development

This chapter examines the skills, competencies, and educational preparation of a mature and effective consultant—internal or external. We present a spectrum of attributes general enough to be applied to any type of consultant and consultation process in any field of work or in any type of client situation. By no means is this an exhaustive study of qualities that a consultant should possess, nor is it a "how to become a consultant" manual. It does represent our experience, ideas, and feelings, mixed in with some research data from practitioners in the consulting field.

There have been so few attempts to classify the competencies of an effective consultant, that the lack has been commented on by Vaill (1971):

> It is difficult to describe consultant skills and abilities, and at the present time it is quite impossible to say how to train persons to practice them. Yet the issue must be addressed if consulting practice is to be effective. (p. 203)[1]

The writer quoted above, Peter B. Vaill, has urged that:

> The critical need now is to collect more data on what these skills and abilities look like . . . and to talk with practitioners in detail, and, where possible, observe them at work, to see if these abilities can be documented. (p. 211)[2]

---

[1] From Peter B. Vaill, "Organization Development: Ten New Dimensions of Practice," in G. Lippitt, L. This, & R. Bidwell (Eds.) *Optimizing Human Resources*. Reading, MA: Addison-Wesley, 1971, pp. 203, 211. Reprinted by permission of author.

[2] See Footnote 1.

One of the difficulties in developing a taxonomy of competencies and skills is the nature of the consultative process as a personal relationship between people trying to solve a problem. A consultant is able to influence this relationship in four ways: by behavioral competence, by communication of helpful concepts and ideas, by degree of acceptance, and by the client's legitimization of the consultant's role. No matter how competent or creative the consultant, the last two factors—acceptance and legitimized role—are essential both to the consultant's opportunity to contribute and actual contribution to problem solution. In this context, the professional behavior of the consultant is of prime importance. In the search for competency, the following criteria might be useful in assessing the consultant (Lippitt, 1969):

1. *Does the consultant form sound interpersonal relations with the client?* A consulting relationship is based on trust developed by effective interpersonal relations. The consultant should allow time for exploring this relationship in sufficient depth so that both parties feel there is the likelihood of developing confidence and trust. Such explorations may take place in a number of ways, but if the consultant asks for an immediate long-range commitment, the client may express reluctance about moving too quickly into such a relationship.

2. *Does the consultant's behavior build the client's independence rather than dependence on the consultant's resources?* Responsible and ethical consultants do not make the client dependent on them. Instead, they recognize the need for people to develop their own competencies and capabilities, while the consultant assists when needed. A consultant can do this without creating dependency.

3. *Does the consultant focus on the problem?* In the realities of consultant-client work, there will be people who feel threatened, upset, and unhappy about the results of any consultation. Consultants who want everyone to like them or to be happy at all times may be insecure. They may dodge a key issue rather than confront the client with corrective measures that are hard to swallow and, thereby, endanger the consultant's continued employment.

4. *Is the consultant nonjudgmental and tolerant toward other consultants and resource disciplines?* Constant derision of the talents of other consultants or disciplines is the behavior of an unprofessional consultant. An effective consultant knows his or her own limitations and sees the value of others' specialties.

5. *Does the consultant respect the confidences of his clients?* Another sign of a professional consultant is the ability to maintain confidentiality concerning dealings with clients. Some consultants attempt

to demonstrate expertise, experience, and profundity by discussing the clients they have served. They may point out ways in which they straightened out other organizations or the times when things went from bad to worse because their advice was not taken. However, a professional does not violate the confidence of individuals or organizations.

6. *Is the consultant clear about contractual arrangements?* Frequently, unprofessional consultants are vague about their fees or the conditions under which they will provide their services. True professionals set ground rules for their work so that a client knows what kind of services will be performed and the rates of pay on an hourly, daily, or job basis.

7. *Does the consultant appropriately achieve influence in the organization?* Another trait of the unprofessional consultant is going around or over the head of the line or staff person who brought the consultant into the organization. While building the consultant's prestige, this creates dependency in the organization and does not develop the capabilities of the persons the consultant was hired to help. Such a consultant does not build the resources of the client.

8. *Does the consultant truthfully indicate the skills he or she possesses that are relative to the client's problem?* One sure sign of a nonprofessional is the consultant who purports to be not only a financial genius, but an expert behavioral scientist, knowledgeable in quantitative methods and all other management sciences. Such a consultant implies that the client has only to tap the consultant's resources on a regular basis to have all the competence needed for running an organization effectively. However, many consultants who are good in one field may not be expert in another. Clients should be wary of consultants who unreasonably imply extensive knowledge and experience; they may be venturing far beyond the limits of their actual skills and abilities.

9. *Does the consultant clearly inform the client concerning the consultant's role and contribution?* Often, an unprofessional consultant will claim to be getting certain work results when he or she actually is not accomplishing that goal at all. The client should remove such a consultant from the premises as quickly as possible. Consultants should clarify their role, including the potentials and limitations inherent in such a clarification.

10. *Does the consultant express willingness to have his or her services evaluated?* Another sign of nonprofessional or amateur consultants is an unwillingness to have their work reviewed or evaluated

by the client system. Clients should exercise caution with a consultant who is reluctant to receive feedback on performance.

11. *Does the consultant participate in a professional association, discipline, or educational process to maintain competency?* Professional resource persons should have ways of continually upgrading their skills and knowledge. Continuing education in a discipline and membership in a professional association are key ways for a consultant to maintain competency and current knowledge.

These common-sense guidelines are based on the experiences we have had in both providing and receiving consulting services. This is, of course, not meant to be an exclusive list, but it indicates some areas in which consultants should develop competency.

CONSULTING COMPETENCIES

Any list of the professional capabilities of a consultant is extensive—something like a combination of the Boy Scouts' laws, requirements for admission to heaven, and the essential elements for securing tenure at an Ivy League college. Nevertheless, we obtained data from thirty-two consultants on their own estimation of key areas of expertise (Lippitt, 1976b). We asked the following three key questions:

1. What are the skills, knowledge, and attitudes that are essential, in your mind, for a person to be able to carry out consultant services, processes, and activities?

2. What do you feel are the educational preparation and learning experiences that would equip a person to be able to function as a mature and effective consultant? (In other words, how could he or she become the person you cited in Question 1?)

3. What criteria can consultants use to evaluate their own effectiveness as it relates to the impact and contribution of their consulting service?

The responses we obtained from the questionnaire were varied, but certain trends were evident. It was obvious that consulting requires a multifaceted group of competencies. As one respondent put it:

> In order to carry out consulting services, processes, and activities effectively, a consultant needs a host of multifaceted skills, knowledge, and attitudes. Some of these attributes are acquired, experienced, and known to the specialist, but I suggest that there are also internal resources, not consciously known to the specialist, that surface from time to time, and are dependent on situational circumstances.

In my experience of trying to develop three different OD teams in recent years, I have not seen any two specialists develop with the same intensity or pattern. This might suggest that we do not have any concrete rules of order that can be draped as the "mold" for a consultant. Those successful specialists that have evolved under my observation (some unsuccessful ones too) always seem to have a special quality that make them credible to the client system. These qualities may be charismatic, professional competence, a flair for the dramatic, a warm personality, or a combination of all of these.

Another respondent listed abilities that are equivalent to competencies of a consultant, as follows:

1. Ability to diagnose a problem;
2. Ability to make an analysis and to interpret the results for the client;
3. Ability to communicate effectively with all types of client system;
4. Ability to help other people become comfortable with change;
5. Ability to maintain and release human energy;
6. Ability to deal with conflict and confrontation;
7. Ability to develop objectives with the client;
8. Ability to help other people learn how to learn;
9. Ability to manage a development and growth effort;
10. Ability to evaluate results;
11. Ability to be proactive;
12. Ability to be creative and innovative in working with the client;
13. Ability of the consultant to be self-renewing.

Another one of our respondents suggested the following:

In my opinion, all the educational preparation and learning experience in the world would not compensate for certain necessary traits and skills of the consultant which do not necessarily come from education. These include:

- Flexibility;
- Innovative and creative ability;
- Ability to quickly and accurately adapt to unfamiliar situations and circumstances;
- Possession of inner motivation, a self-starter;
- Extreme perception and sensitivity towards others;
- Ability to deal successfully with ambiguity;
- Extreme honesty, ethics of the profession;
- Genuine desire to help others;

- Profound respect for self;
- Optimism and self-confidence;
- Sincerity; and
- Charisma.

With these traits or characteristics, individuals have a much greater chance for success in the field of consulting than they would without them.

Summary of Consultant Competencies

When we summarized the responses from the thirty-two consultants, the competencies of a consultant seemed to cluster as follows:

KNOWLEDGE AREAS

1. Thorough grounding in the behavioral sciences;
2. An equally thorough foundation in the administrative philosophies, policies, and practices of organizational systems and larger social systems;
3. Knowledge of educational and training methodologies, especially laboratory methods, problem-solving exercises, and role playing;
4. An understanding of the stages in the growth of individuals, groups, organizations, and communities and how social systems function at different stages;
5. Knowledge of how to design and help a change process;
6. Knowledge and understanding of human personality, attitude formation, and change;
7. Knowledge of oneself: motivations, strengths, weaknesses, and biases;
8. An understanding of the leading philosophical systems as a framework for thought and a foundation for value system.

SKILL AREAS

1. Communication skills: listening, observing, identifying, and reporting;
2. Teaching and persuasive skills: ability to effectively impart new ideas and insights and to design learning experiences that contribute to growth and change;
3. Counseling skills to help others reach meaningful decisions on their own power;

4. Ability to form relationships based on trust and to work with a great variety of persons of different backgrounds and personalities; sensitivity to the feelings of others; ability to develop and share one's own charisma;

5. Ability to work with groups and teams in planning and implementing change; skill in using group-dynamics techniques and laboratory training methods;

6. Ability to utilize a variety of intervention methods and the ability to determine which intervention is most appropriate at a given time;

7. Skill in designing surveys, interviewing, and other data-collection methods;

8. Ability to diagnose problems with a client, to locate sources of help, power, and influence, to understand a client's values and culture, and to determine readiness for change;

9. Ability to be flexible in dealing with all types of situations;

10. Skill in using problem-solving techniques and in assisting others in problem solving.

ATTITUDE AREAS

1. Attitude of a professional: competence, integrity, feeling of responsibility for helping clients cope with their problems;

2. Maturity: self-confidence, courage to stand by one's views, willingness to take necessary risks, ability to cope with rejection, hostility, and suspicion;

3. Open-mindedness, honesty, intelligence;

4. Possession of a humanistic value system: belief in the importance of the individual; belief in technology and efficiency as means and not ends; trust in people and the democratic process in economic activities.

Such a summary is one step toward identifying competencies.

A Taxonomy of Change-Agent Skills

Menzel (1975) developed a helpful list of skills entitled A Taxonomy of Change-Agent Skills (see Figure 6). Menzel related his taxonomy to four key roles and phases of planned change, and he listed some twenty-five skill areas in his model.

The Process of Planned Change: — ROLES	CHANGE AGENT SKILL AREAS	UN-FREEZING		MOVEMENT			RE-FREEZING	
PHASES OF PLANNED CHANGE		1. Awareness of Need for Change	2. Establish Change Relationship	3. Diagnosis of System Problems	4. Examine Options; Set Goals	5. Acceptance; Take Action	6. Generalization and Stabilization	7. Termination
EDUCATING	Researcher			X	X	XX		
	Writer	X			X	X		
	Designer			X	XX		X	
	Teacher			X		X		X
	Instructor					X	X	X
	Trainer				X	X	XX	X
	Advocate	XR			XR	XR	X	XR
	Conference Leader	X			X	XX	X	X
	Life/Career Planner				X	X		
DIAGNOSING	Action Researcher	X		XX	XX	X	X	
	Writer			XX				
	Diagnoser	X		XX	X	X	X	X
	Instrument/Survey Designer			XX				
	Data Analyst	X		XX	X	X	X	X
	Evaluator			X	X	XX	XX	X
CONSULTING	Role Model	X	XX	X	X			XX
	Relater at all levels	X	XX	X	X	X	X	X
	Expert in Consulting Processes:							
	Survey Feedback	X			XX	XX	X	X
	Process Observation	X			XX	X	X	X
	Decision Making			X	X	XX		X
	Problem Solving	XX			XX	XX	X	X
	Conflict Resolution	X			XX	XX	X	X
	Conference Leadership	X		X	X	XX	X	X
	Confronter	XR			XR		XR	XR
	Intervenor					XX	XX	X
	Systems Analyst	X			XX	XX	X	
	Designer/Planner	X			X	XX	X	
	Adapter			X	X	XX	X	XX
LINKING	Resourcer Linker		X	X	XX	XX	X	XX
	Internal Resources	X	XX	XX	XX	XX	XX	XX
	External Resources							
	Special Services				X	X	XX	
	In "thin" areas			(wherever help is indicated or needed)				
	Experts/Theorists							
	for Action Research			X	X	X	X	
	Referrer	X				XX		XX

Code: **X**-Relevant   **XX**-Especially Relevant   **XR**-Relevant but Risky

Figure 6. A taxonomy of change agent skills
(From Robert K. Menzel, "A Taxonomy of Change Agent Skills," in *The Journal of European Training*, 1975, *4*(5), pp. 289-291. Reprinted by permission of the publisher.)

Menzel (1975, pp. 290-291)[3] explains his list of skills as follows:

CHANGE-AGENT SKILL	EXPLANATION
Educating	
Researcher	Familiar with the theoretical bases for change
Writer	Able to write clearly and persuasively
Designer	Can design educational workshops and events
Teacher	Successful in helping others to learn
Instructor	Teaching related more to "training" tasks
Trainer	Beyond traditional "training"; able to "laboratory train," using heuristic methods
Advocate	Holding out for a point of view or plan of action
Conference Leader	Able to lead, and teach others to lead, a participative meeting or conference
Life/Career Planner	Able to help clients plan careers
Diagnosing	
Action Researcher	Knows how to utilize research and survey data and systems theory to apply to present situation in the organization
Diagnoser	Ability to identify what needs to be analyzed, what data gathered, how to obtain and use them
Survey Designer	Can get needed data in simplest way
Data Analyst	Can draw correct conclusions from data and prepare them for presentation to client
Evaluator	Uses evaluation as an on-going process
Consulting	
Role Model	Can practice what he preaches; congruent
Relater	Uses interpersonal skills to maintain credibility with all levels of organization
Expert in Processes	Possesses expertise in change agent's tools of the trade. Examples listed in the matrix; although also interventions, each requires "skills which have to be learned"
Confronter	Able to face issues and people head-on

---

[3]From Robert K. Menzel, "A Taxonomy of Change Agent Skills," in *The Journal of European Training*, 1975, 4(5), pp. 289-291. Reprinted by permission of the publisher.

CHANGE-AGENT SKILL	EXPLANATION
Systems Analyst	Can employ systems approach to change process
Intervenor	Can use his expanding repertoire of interventions appropriately and effectively
Designer/Planner	Can plan and design and execute interventions forcefully
Adapter	Applies his own experience and that of others in a creative and relevant way
Linking	
Resourcer Linker	Skill in linking the best resourcers with the correctly identified need
Internal	Identifies, enlists, trains, and employs resourcers within the organization to effect change
External	Identifies appropriate external resourcers, facilitates their entry and effective functioning. Uses internal-external consultant relationship well
Special tactics	
Where internal CA lacks skills or credibility	Three examples of linking functions where CA skills are employed
Theorist-experts for action research	
Referrer	Able to assist client in employment of resourcers who do not require CA's involvement

In his definition of the four roles, Menzel identifies consulting as separate from educating, diagnosing, and linking. As indicated in Chapter 3, we feel those roles are *included* in the multiple functions of the consultant.

Qualities of a Consultant

It seems to us that the qualities needed by a consultant fall into two broad categories: (1) intellectual abilities and (2) behavioral competencies.

Intellectually, the consultant needs what we call the ability to make a *dilemma analysis*, because a client who calls in an outside consultant is probably faced with a situation that appears insoluble, or at least puzzling and difficult. The consultant must recognize that a dilemma, whether real or not, does exist in the minds of those requesting help. The consultant's role is to discover the nature of the dilemma and to help determine what really is causing it.

To cope with dilemmas (either real or not), the consultant must have a special type of diagnostic skill and, as we indicated in Chapter 4, the consulting process itself creates additional dilemmas. It is only through skillful examination of the client situation that a consultant can see the relationships between various subsystems and the interdependent nature of individuals, groups, and the environmental setting of the consultation.

Insight, perception, and intuition are necessary in order to make multiple dilemma analyses. Insight and perception are vital because the problem and the solution of almost any dilemma are part of a very complex situation. The consultant's toughest task is to penetrate the complexity and isolate the key situational variables. Unless the important factors can be sifted from the maze of detail, and the causes are separated from the symptoms, accurate diagnosis is impossible.

In addition to diagnostic abilities, the consultant needs implementation skills. Obviously, a consultant must have some basic knowledge of the behavioral sciences and the theories and methods of the consulting discipline. But, more than these, the consultant needs imagination and experimental flexibility. In consultation, dissolving a dilemma is essentially a creative process. No real situation is going to fit perfectly the mold suggested by typical techniques or textbook methods. Diversity and unique circumstances almost always exist. Consultants must be imaginative enough to innovate adaptations and tailor their concepts to meet real demands. It is vital for consultants to be able to envision the impact or ultimate outcome of the actions they propose or implement. But, like most things, their work is as much a process of experimental trial and error as it is a matter of *a priori* solutions. The courage to experiment and the flexibility to try as many approaches as needed to solve the problem are important ingredients in the practitioner's make-up.

The other major qualities of the consultant are what we call interpersonal attributes. Above all, consultants must be professional in attitude and behavior. To be successful, the consultant must be as sincerely interested in helping the client as any good doctor is interested in helping the patient. If the practitioner is primarily concerned with making a large fee or displaying competence as an internal staff member, and is only secondarily interested in helping the client, then the client will soon recognize and deal with such a person accordingly. People in trouble are not fools. They can sense objectivity, honesty, and, above all, integrity. One of our consultant respondents put it as follows:

> Perhaps primary to the role of a consultant is interpersonal skill. There are, of course, many variegations of interpersonal competence. This is one skill

that quickly identifies you with the client system. Usually it is the first skill tested and continues to be tested throughout the relationship with the client . . . It involves creating conditions of psychological success, of being creative in arranging knowledge gained with the client, an ability to develop conceptual models to explain or relate certain situations, an ability to exude and gain trust, an ability to recognize and handle conflict, etc. These skills and knowledges are ever evolving in a consultant.

After surveying the thirty-two consultants, we noted that all the responses emphasized the importance of the consultant having self-insight. As one respondent stated:

Above all, consultants must be able to come to grips with themselves. Whatever views one may have of the client system necessarily interface with one's own value system, perceptions, and attitudes. Thus, consultants must be able to associate or disassociate their own internal constraints from those activities of the client.

Stanley M. Herman (1974), a well-known internal consultant, expressed this very well in the following poem:

FREEDOM

No one grants you freedom
You are free if you are free

No one enthralls you
You enthrall yourself
And when you have
You may hand your tether
   to another
   to many others
   to all others, or
   to yourself

Perhaps the last is worst of all
For that slave master is hardest to see
And hardest to rebel against
But he is easiest to hate
   and to damage

I do not know how to tell you to be free
I wish I did
But I do know some signs of freedom

One is in doing what you want to do
  Though someone tells you not to
Another is in doing what you want to do
  even though someone tells you to do it. (p. 246)[4]

A consultant who is entering a client system needs a strong tolerance for ambiguity. From our experience, one's first acquaintance with a client can be marked by a certain amount of bewilderment. It takes time to figure out the situation, and during this time one is going to experience a certain amount of confusion, as we indicated in Chapter 2 when discussing the entry phase. The consultant must expect this to occur and not be worried by it.

Coupled with the consultant's tolerance for ambiguity must be patience and a high frustration level. Helping a client to find goals and solve problems is likely to be a long and confronting experience. Quick results, full cooperation, and complete success are unlikely.

If people think they may be adversely affected, they usually will respond to attempts to change their relationships and behavior patterns with resistance or dependency, resentment or overenthusiasm, and obstructionism or rationalization. It is important for consultants to be mature and realistic enough to recognize that many of their actions and hopes for change are going to be frustrated. Such maturity is necessary to avoid reacting with the defeatism and withdrawal that commonly accompanies the frustration of a person's sincere efforts to help others.

The consultant who objectively concludes that he or she cannot help the client system should, of course, withdraw and if possible, refer the client to some other source of professional help. This act also requires maturity.

In summary, we are suggesting that the consultant should have a stable personality, conceptual sophistication, good interpersonal skills, and a good sense of timing. Timing can be crucial. The best conceived and articulated plans for change can be destroyed if introduced at the wrong time. Timing is linked to a knowledge of the client, to the realities of the consulting situation, and to the kind of patience that overrides one's enthusiasm for wanting to try out a newly conceived alternative.

---

[4]Reprinted from J. William Pfeiffer and John E. Jones (Eds.). *The 1974 Annual Handbook for Group Facilitators.* La Jolla, Calif.: University Associates, 1974.

Obviously, consulting involves people dealing with people, more than people dealing with machines or mathematical solutions. Consultants must have good interpersonal skills. They must be able to communicate and deal with people in an atmosphere of tact, trust, politeness, friendliness, and stability. This is important because the impact of the practitioner's personality must be minimized enough to keep it from becoming another variable in the existential setting and contributing to the existing complexity. Beyond this, a consultant's success will depend on persuasiveness and tact in handling the interpersonal contact on which the change effort is based. Because such an array of skills and competencies is not easily achieved, each consultant should continue to evaluate his or her own skill and style. Havelock (1973) states:

> Most of the tactics or functions discussed (as interventions) cannot simply be picked up casually from a manual. *They are skills which have to be learned.* A good tactic badly executed may be worse than no tactic at all. (p. 153)[5]

EDUCATION AND DEVELOPMENT OF CONSULTANTS

What is being done to train, educate, and develop consultants? This is a difficult question, one with which we have been concerned in our practice during the past twenty-five years.

Unfortunately, the training and development of consultants has been a haphazard process. Only recently have workshops and courses for developing consultant skills appeared. In commenting on these workshops (for educational consulting) we (Lippitt, 1971) have pointed out the following:

> In laboratories on consultation skills for professionals of all types, some of the problems most frequently focused on for practice include how to:
>
> • Stimulate a need for help;
> • Give a taste of what it might be like to work together;
> • Develop a contract of collaboration;
> • Involve the appropriate client group;
> • Be supportive of working through resistance;
> • Stimulate change objectives or images of potentiality;
> • Get feedback to guide a consultation;

---

[5] From R. G. Havelock, *The Change Agent's Guide to Innovation in Education*. Englewood Cliffs, NJ: Educational Technology Publications, 1973, p. 153. Reprinted by permission of the publisher.

- Conceptualize criteria for making choices among alternative interventions.

It is a heartening sign that more and more professional helpers are accepting the idea that they also need help in practicing the specific interpersonal skills of intervention and designing consultation situations. (p. 2)[6]

Some of our questionnaire respondents suggested the acquisition of quite an array of formal education, as indicated by the following:

I think the key to the preparation of consultants is a *mixed background* of *interdisciplinary education and experience*. It seems almost mandatory that they should have university training in some discipline and preferably several disciplines. A wide variety of disciplines can serve as basic training: psychiatry, general psychology, social psychology, education, political science, sociology, anthropology, business administration, or other of the behavioral sciences. What is important is that the practitioner have a working knowledge of many of these disciplines. It would also be desirable for him to have some knowledge of the technical disciplines such as operations research, general systems theory, finance, cybernetics, etc. In other words, a rather broad educational background with as much mix as possible, balanced against enough in-depth training in certain fields to have a very solid academic foundation in at least a few fields. The whole purpose of the mixed interdiscipline approach is to give breadth and scope to the practitioner, rather than narrow specialization. The problems involved in consultation tend to be interdisciplinary in character and not narrow. Thus, broad knowledge and multiple skills are needed.

Another consultant/practitioner emphasized both the formal and informal nature of the educational development of the consultant:

I have concluded that a careful and rather precise developmental plan of education, training, and experience is required for consultants. It is the rare individual who acquires all of the ingredients necessary by happenstance.

First, I would seek out those professionals (Argyris, Beckhard, Bennis, the Lippitt brothers, F. Mann, Shepard, Schmidt, Tannenbaum, etc.) who are actively conducting, teaching, or coaching formal seminars or programs in consulting skills, conflict resolution, group dynamics, etc. These references not only have the appropriate academic reputation, but also have practical consulting experience with organizations. Studying or working with such persons would be invaluable.

Second, I would engage in a self-designed "readings" program. This would include not only an updating of selected texts, articles, and research papers, but also contemporary journals, papers, and magazines.

---

[6]Reprinted with permission of Social Sciences Education Consortium, Inc., Boulder, Colorado 80302.

Third, I would join the NTL OD Network, ASTD, ORI Network, or similar groups, and participate in discussions, review of presentations, and exchanging experiences and papers.

Fourth, I would try to critique or make an assessment of my own strengths, attitudes, weaknesses, etc., and formulate a plan to strengthen my skills and knowledge along the lines outlined above.

Fifth, I would work at it. This means to actually take on different consultant roles with clients or join with another consultant. There isn't anything quite so valuable as residential learning experiences to stimulate personal growth as an intervener.

Sixth, I would attend a variety of professional conferences, laboratory sessions and special programs like the NTL/Bethel OD Program, the UCLA Behavioral Development Program, ITORP, etc.

In summary then, there are formal possibilities in behavioral science with universities and professional organizations which can help in preparation, but perhaps personal commitment to learn stands above all.

One respondent (Naismith, 1971) developed an interesting matrix of informal and formal learning experiences as related to the needed skills, knowledge, and attitudes of consultants (see Figure 7).

We agree with one comment made by eleven of the thirty-two respondents to our questionnaire. They indicated that an effective consultant should have had experience as a line manager or leader with a group, organization, or community. Such experience gives depth, reality, and insight to one's role as a consultant in coping with real problems, group decisions, organizational realities, and/or community conflict. As one experienced consultant (Beckhard, 1971) put it:

> Help is never really help unless and until it is perceived as "helpful" by the person on the receiving end—regardless of the good intention or reputation of the helper or consultant. (p. 2)[7]

It does require considerable knowledge and skill, as well as a flexibility of response, to be a professional consultant. As Schmidt (1970) puts it:

> For there is a time to confront but also a time to reduce tension:
>
> A time to use power but also a time to use persuasion.
>
> A time to act but also a time to diagnose.
>
> A time to accelerate change but also a time to slow it down.
>
> A time to intervene but also a time to refrain from intervening.

---

[7]From Richard Beckhard, *The Leader Looks at the Consultative Process.* Washington, D.C.: Leadership Resources, Inc., 1971, p. 2. Reprinted by permission of the publisher.

CHARACTERISTICS OF THE OD PRACTITIONER	MEANS OF ACQUIRING NEEDED CHARACTERISTICS							
	FORMAL EDUCATION					INFORMAL LEARNING EXPERIENCES		
	Literature of Behavioral Science and Organizations	Tutorial Under Experienced Practitioner	Individual Therapy and Sensitivity Training	Training Labs	University Courses in OD	Experience; Exposure to Organizations	Discussion with Peers	Experimentation
SKILLS/ABILITY TO:								
1. Use scientific methodology	X				X	X		X
2. Deal with people and situations; take action		X	X	X		X		X
3. Teach; communicate	X	X	X	X		X		
4. Diagnose and sense organizational problems		X	X	X		X		
5. Cope with political realities	X					X		
6. Detect success/failure			X	X		X		X
KNOWLEDGE OF:								
1. Change theory	X	X				X		
2. Characteristics of organic systems	X					X	X	
3. Self			X	X			X	
4. A plan, conceptual model, or framework	X					X	X	
5. Specific OD methods	X	X				X		
6. Research tools	X	X				X		X
7. Organizational environment	X					X	X	
ATTITUDES:								
1. Trust; openness			X	X			X	
2. Flexibility, adaptability, learning			X	X		X		X
3. Desire to help			X	X				
4. Honesty with self and others			X	X				

Figure 7. Educational opportunities and consulting skills
(Adapted from D. Naismith)

But whether we confront or collaborate, intervene or analyze, let it flow from understanding and courage and love and not from ignorance and cowardice and fear—for these cannot long survive on any frontier. (p. 4)[8]

In his reference to a frontier, Schmidt is referring to the organizational frontier facing the postindustrial society. Such a frontier is going to require all the excellence that multiple-discipline consultants and leaders can bring to bear on complex and unknown problems. The challenge to those of us who dare to help both ourselves and others to cope with this frontier is clearly expressed by Schmidt (1970):

> Those who would live creatively and usefully at the frontier need now and then to pause and ask themselves:
>
> Am I prepared to live with uncertainty—to move before all the facts are in (they never are) or arranged in clear patterns (they seldom are)?
>
> Am I willing to risk a failure from acting now on the basis of my best judgement rather than waiting for others to take the first chance?
>
> Can I stay open to new learning from every experience—my own and others?
>
> Can I continue, even in crisis, to remember the humanness of those whose lives I touch—whether they view things my way or not? (p. 4)[9]

If there are consultants with these kinds of values, attitudes, and beliefs, they may yet reinstitute a confidence in all consultants as fellow human beings whose help can provide mutual growth for both parties in a consulting relationship.

---

[8] From W. H. Schmidt, *Organizational Frontiers and Human Values*. Belmont, CA: Wadsworth Publishing Company, Inc., 1970, p. 4. Reprinted by permission of the publisher.

[9] See Footnote 8.

References and Suggested Reading

Academy of Management. Proposed code of ethics. *Organization Development Division Newsletter*, Winter 1976.

American Psychological Association. *Casebook on ethical standards of psychologists*. Washington, D.C.: Author, 1967.

American Society for Training and Development. Code of ethics. *Who's Who in Training and Development*, November 1975, 30.

Association of Consulting Management Engineers, Inc. *Ethics and professional conduct in management consulting*. New York: Author, 1966.

Association of Consulting Management Engineers, Inc. *Professional practices in management consulting*. New York: Author, 1966.

Argyris, C. Explorations in consulting-client relationships. *Human Organization*, 1961, *20*, 121-133.

Argyris, C. Dangers in applying results from experimental social psychology. *American Psychologist*, 1975, *30*, 469-485.

Bancroft, J. F. Activating a code of ethics. *Personnel and Guidance Journal*, 1971, *50*(4), 260.

Banet, A. G., Jr. Consultation-skills inventory. In J. W. Pfeiffer & J. E. Jones (Eds.), *The 1976 annual handbook for group facilitators*. La Jolla, CA: University Associates, 1976.

Beck, C. E. Ethical practice: Foundations and emerging issues. *Personnel and Guidance Journal*, December 1971, 321.

Beckhard, R. *Organization development*. Reading, MA: Addison-Wesley, 1969.

Beckhard, R. *The leader looks at the consultative process* (Rev. ed.). Falls Church, VA: Leadership Resources, Inc., 1971.

Benne, K. D. Some ethical problems in group and organizational consultation. *Journal of Social Issues*, 1959, *15*(2), 60-67.

ↄpplying behavioral science to planned
꠸. Kayser, *Changing organizational*
꠸-Hall, 1973, 73-75.

sultants and clients to research on
paper, George Washington Univer-

Campbell, S. Graduate programs in applied behavioral science: A directory. In J. W. Pfeiffer & J. E. Jones (Eds.), *The 1978 annual handbook for group facilitators*. La Jolla, CA: University Associates, 1978.

Clark, P. A. *Action research and organizational change*. New York: Harper & Row, 1972.

Collier, A. T. *Management, man, and values*. New York: Harper & Row, 1962.

Committee on Scientific and Professional Ethics and Conduct. Rules and procedures. *American Psychologist*, 1968, *23*(5).

Dekom, A. K. *The internal consultant* (Research study 101). New York: American Management Association, 1969.

Festinger, L. *Research methods in the behavioral sciences*. New York: The Dryden Press, 1953.

Fletcher, J. *The situation ethics debate*. Philadelphia: The Westminister Press, 1968.

French, W. L., & Bell, C. H., Jr. *Organization development: Behavioral science interventions for organization improvement*. Englewood Cliffs, NJ: Prentice-Hall, 1973.

Frohman, M. A., Sashkin, M., & Kavanagh, M. J. Action research as applied to organization development. In S. Lee Spray (Ed.), *Organizational effectiveness*. Kent, OH: Kent State University Press, 1976.

Gibb, J. R., & Lippitt, R. (Eds.) Consulting with groups and organizations. *Journal of Social Issues*, 1959, *15*(2).

Golembiewski, R. T. *Men, management and morality: Toward a new organizational ethic*. New York: McGraw-Hill, 1965.

Golightly, C. L. A philosopher's view of values and ethics. *Personnel and Guidance Journal*, December, 1971, 289.

Greiner, L. E. Red flags in organization development. *Business Horizons*, 1972, *15*(3), 17-24.

Havelock, R. G. *The change agents' guide to innovation in education*. Englewood Cliffs, NJ: Educational Technology Publications, 1973.

Havelock, R. G., & Havelock, M. C. *Training for change agents*. Ann Arbor, MI: Institute for Social Research, 1973.

Herman, S. M. Freedom. In J. W. Pfeiffer & J. E. Jones (Eds.), *The 1974 annual handbook for group facilitators*. La Jolla, CA: University Associates, 1974.

Holland, P. *Ethics and the consultant*. Unpublished student paper, George Washington University, 1972.

Hollander, S. C. (compiler). *Management consultants and clients*. East Lansing, MI: Michigan State University Press, 1972.

Huse, E. F. *Organization development and change*. St. Paul: West, 1976.

Jenks, R. S. An action-research approach to organizational change. In W. W. Burke & M. A. Hornstein (Eds.), *The social technology of organization development*. La Jolla, CA: University Associates, 1972.

Kaplan, A. *The conduct of inquiry*. San Francisco: Chandler, 1964.

Kelman, H. C. Manipulation of human behavior: An ethical dilemma for the social scientist. *Journal of Social Issues*, 1965, *21*(2), 31-46. Also in W. G. Bennis, K. D. Benne, & R. Chin (Eds.), *The planning of change* (2nd. ed.). New York: Holt, Rinehart and Winston, 1969.

Kubr, M. (Ed.) *Management consulting: A guide to the profession*. Geneva: International Labour Office, 1976.

Lawrence, P. R., & Lorsch, J. D., *Developing organizations: Diagnosis and action*. Reading, MA: Addison-Wesley, 1969.

Lewin, K. Research center for group dynamics. *Sociometry*, 1945, *8*(2), 9.

Lippitt, G. L. A study of the consultation process. *Journal of Social Issues*, 1959, *15*(2), 43-50.

Lippitt, G. L. *Value implications in organization renewal, ethical guidelines for leadership*. Washington, D.C.: Project Associates, 1968.

Lippitt, G. L. *Organization renewal*. Englewood Cliffs, NJ: Prentice-Hall, 1969.

Lippitt, G. L. Criteria for selecting, evaluating, and developing consultants. *Training and Development Journal*, 1972, *26*(8), 12-17

Lippitt, G. L. *A competency-based survey of consultant skills*. Unpublished study, George Washington University, 1976. (b)

Lippitt, G. L., & Lippitt, R. The consulting process in action. In J. E. Jones & J. W. Pfeiffer (Eds.), *The 1977 annual handbook for group facilitators*. La Jolla, CA: University Associates, 1977.

Lippitt, G. L., & This, L. ITORP· Implementing the organization renewal process. *Training and Development Journal*, 1970, *24*(7), 10-15.

Lippitt, R. *Value-judgment problems of the social scientist participating in action-research*. Paper presented at the annual meeting of the American Psychological Association, September, 1950.

Lippitt, R. Dimensions of the consultant's job. *Journal of Social Issues*, 1959, *15*(2), 5-12.

Lippitt, R. On finding, using, and being a consultant. *Social Science Education Consortium Newsletter*, November 1971, 2.

Margulies, N., & Raia, A. *Organization development; Values, process, and technology.* New York: McGraw-Hill, 1972.

Maslow, A. H. *Eupsychian management.* Homewood, IL: Richard D. Irwin, 1965.

Menzel, R. K. A taxonomy of change-agent skills. *Journal of European Training,* 1975, *4*(5), 287-288.

Naismith, D. Unpublished response to G. Lippitt. George Washington University, Fall 1971.

Organization Renewal, Inc. *Organization renewal work conference* (ITORP) (Rev.). Washington, D.C., 1973.

Pfeiffer, J. W., & Jones, J. E. Co-facilitating. In J. E. Jones & J. W. Pfeiffer (Eds.) *The 1975 annual handbook for group facilitators.* La Jolla, CA: University Associates, 1975.

Pfeiffer, J. W., & Jones, J. E. Ethical considerations in consulting. In J. E. Jones & J. W. Pfeiffer (Eds.), *The 1977 annual handbook for group facilitators.* La Jolla, CA: University Associates, 1977.

Pfeiffer, J. W., & Jones, J. E. (Eds.) *The 1978 annual handbook for group facilitators.* La Jolla, CA: University Associates, 1978.

Redel, F. *Diagnosing teacher training needs.* Unpublished document, 1941.

Roberts, M. W. *Action research—An OD technology.* Unpublished paper, George Washington University, 1975.

Rosenberg, P. P. *An experimental analysis of psychodrama.* Unpublished doctoral dissertation. Harvard University, 1951.

Sashkin, M. Models and roles of change agents. In J. W. Pfeiffer & J. E. Jones (Eds.), *The 1974 annual handbook for group facilitators.* La Jolla, CA: University Associates, 1974.

Schmidt, W. H. (Ed.) *Organizational frontiers and human values.* Belmont, CA: Wadsworth, 1970.

Schmithorst, J. *The ethical dilemma in consulting.* Unpublished student paper, George Washington University, 1974.

Shay, P. W. Ethics and professional practices in management consulting. *Advanced Management Journal,* 1965, *30*(1), 13-20.

Spier, S. S. Kurt Lewin's "force field analysis." In J. E. Jones & J. W. Pfeiffer (Eds.), *The 1973 annual handbook for group facilitators.* La Jolla, CA: University Associates 1973.

Steele, F. Consultants and detectives. *Journal of Applied Behavioral Science,* 1969, *5*(2), 201.

Swartz, D., & Lippitt, G. Evaluating the consulting process. *Journal of European Training,* 1975, *4*(5), 310.

Tichy, N., & Nisberg, J. N. Change agent bias: What they view determines what they do. *Group & Organization Studies: The International Journal for Group Facilitators,* 1976, *1*(3), 286-301.

Vaill, P. B. Organization development: Ten new dimensions of practice. In G. Lippitt, L. This, R. Bidwell (Eds.), *Optimizing human resources*. Reading, MA: Addison-Wesley, 1971, 203-212.

Walton, R. E., & Warwick, D. P. The ethics of organization development. *Journal of Applied Behavioral Science*, 1973, 9(6), 681-698.

Weisbord, M. R. Organizational diagnosis: Six places to look for trouble with or without a theory. *Group & Organization Studies: The International Journal for Group Facilitators*, 1976, 1(4), 430-447.

Annotated Bibliography

Argyris, C. *Intervention theory and method: A behavioral science view*. Reading, MA: Addison-Wesley, 1970, 379 pp.

This book evaluates the methods by which organizational intervention can be made effective, and it presents a theory of consulting. In Part One, "Theory and Method," the author discusses the goals of intervention, conditions under which decisions can be made, resources used to solve problems, implications of organizational deficiencies and ways to overcome them, research-related issues, and applications. Part Two contains a sequence of case illustrations of issues that must be dealt with in order to assure continuity within a total development effort.

Blake, R. R. & Mouton, J. S. *Consultation*. Reading, MA: Addison-Wesley, 1976, 484 pp.

This book explores the field of consultation in terms of theory and practice, with emphasis on the various consultation approaches and their underlying dynamics in resolving problems. A unique feature of the text is the Consulcube®, a systematic framework that helps identify the kinds of consultation that should be offered under specified and definable conditions.

Carkhuff, R. R. *Helping and human relations: A primer for lay and professional helpers* (Vol. 1). New York: Holt, Rinehart and Winston, 1969, 334 pp.

The author presents the three Rs of helping—right, responsibility, and role—which are complemented by a fourth: realization. Literature on current treatment processes, as well as the results of the ongoing search for effective models in helping, are presented. The book assumes that readers have some prior knowledge in the field of counseling and psychotherapy.

Dyer, W. G. *Insight to impact: Strategies for interpersonal and organizational change* (Rev. ed.). Salt Lake City, UT: Brigham Street House, 1976, 200 pp.

This is a revised edition of the author's earlier work; sixteen chapters have been amended and expanded, and nine completely new chapters have been added. Sections explore such subjects as the planning and implementation of organizational change, common organizational conditions that discourage or

114

oppose change, how to remove change barriers with effective change plans, and the nature of effective training as a means to constructive change.

Egan, G. *The skilled helper: A model for systematic helping and interpersonal relating*. Monterey, CA: Brooks/Cole, 1975, 258 pp.
Egan applies the technique of task analysis to the helping process and the helper-helpee relationship. First, he identifies tasks to be accomplished; second, skills needed to accomplish these tasks; and third, the training approach that is best for acquiring these skills. In a practical working model, he describes distinct stages through which helper and helpee progress

Lippitt, G. L. *Visualizing change*. La Jolla, CA: University Associates, 1973, 370 pp.
This book deals in practical, straightforward, uncomplicated terms with the essential theory, techniques, and requirements of model-building in the applied behavioral sciences. The author applies model-building technology to various levels of human behavior including the individual, the small group, and the organization. He provides a practical set of guidelines and methods for enhancing and harnessing unused creativity in the human systems area. The principles discussed in the book are illustrated with over 137 models.

Lippitt, G. L. (Ed.) *The role of the training director as an internal consultant*. Special issue of *The Journal of European Training*, 1976, 96 pp. Available in the United States from Development Publications, Washington, D.C. 20016.(a)
A group of original articles written by seven of the foremost experts in consultation. Each author has served as both an internal and external consultant. They present guidelines for the internal consultant as well as skill application examples.

Lippitt, R., Watson, J., & Westley, B. *The dynamics of planned change: A comparative study of principles and techniques*. New York: Harcourt Brace Jovanovich, 1958.
A classic in the field, this book discusses the role of the *change agent* in terms of stages in the process of change. It gives examples with different client systems—individual, group, organization, and community. The authors provide helpful guidelines to cope with resistance to change.

Schein, E. A. *Process consultation: Its role in organization development*. Reading, MA: Addison-Wesley, 1969, 148 pp.
This clearly written book introduces and explains the theory and practice of process consultation by focusing on the moment-to-moment behavior of the consultant rather than on the overall design of the program. Case studies are used throughout the book as illustrations of process consultation.

Steele, F. *Consulting for organizational change*. Amherst, MA: University of Massachusetts Press, 1975, 200 pp.
This book is a readable, informative, and thought-provoking account of the less publicized functions and techniques of the consultant. It emphasizes the

learning phases of consultation for both the client(s) and the consultant(s). The author points out the potential errors and hazards of being a consultant for change, whether practicing alone or in teams. All phases of the consultation process are covered, from the beginnings of a consultant-client relationship, through the establishment of proper environments and attitudes for the helping relationship, to the closeout times of reflection and learning by the consultant about the helping process itself.

Walton, R. E. *Interpersonal peacemaking: Confrontations and third-party consultation.* Reading, MA: Addison-Wesley, 1969, 152 pp.

This book is directed toward behavioral science consultants and other individuals involved in third-party consultation. It presents a model for diagnosing recurrent conflict between two persons. Based on the author's understanding of the dynamics of interpersonal conflict episodes, the book includes a number of strategic third-party functions that can facilitate a constructive confrontation.

Appendix A
Suggestions for Continued Learning

The reader probably shares our experience that internalizing new concepts and converting ideas and intentions into an available repertoire of behavior requires time and testing and, most of all, the support of interaction while learning with others.

We strongly recommend that consultants develop some strategies and a design for their continuing growth as skilled helpers. Here are some of the strategies we have found helpful and have observed as successful supports for colleagues and students.

GETTING FEEDBACK FROM HELPEES

A basic strategy of consulting and a great source of professional growth is the practice of collecting feedback data from those you are trying to serve. We use some type of feedback tool as a part of every contact, for example, at the end of every meeting, at the end of a consultation session, or at the end of a day of work with a client system. This instrument may take only ten minutes to fill out; it is usually two or three scales with some comments. As an alternative, one may take the last fifteen minutes of a session for a review and to set up an agenda, e.g., "Let's review how things have gone. I'd especially like to get comments on your feelings about my efforts to be helpful. As you think about it right now, what was helpful and not so helpful? How might we work together differently next time?"

Of course, it is crucial at the next session to share what you perceived from the feedback responses and how you intend to utilize it. In our experience, there is no better way to build an effective working relationship.

CO-TRAINING AND CO-CONSULTING

Another great source of support and stimulus to a consultant's growth is to team with a colleague, either as a peer or as an apprentice (Pfeiffer & Jones, 1975). This requires planning together, which means sharing, testing, modifying, defending, and articulating values, concepts, rationale, designs, and techniques. Additionally, there is the opportunity to observe the performance of someone else, elicit feedback observations about one's own performance, debrief each other and learn from the shared experience. We hope you create and utilize as many opportunities as you can for this source of continuing growth.

DOCUMENTATION, PUBLICATION, PRESENTATION

We should adopt as a goal the sharing of our discoveries and learnings with others. This is valuable because it is one of the most effective procedures for personal growth, a pathway to recognition by others, and a contribution to the practice of helping.

Several activities assist in this area of growth. First, it is important to plan for the documentation of what you do as a trainer or as a consultant. Sometimes you can arrange for others to take notes, or you may want to write notes immediately after a session or record some verbal action on tape.

Another important thing is to think and act as though the record of what you are doing will be useful and important information to share. It helps, therefore, to have committed yourself to the preparation of a report, publication, or a presentation concerning your learnings.

Again, as in co-consulting, there is value in a commitment to share the writing effort. This supports your motivation, makes the task more interesting, and the division of labor makes it easier to document and to write. The book you are reading is an example of this suggestion.

ASKING OTHERS

Most of us are inhibited in expressing curiosity about what our colleagues do and how they do it. However, this curiosity reflects a desire to learn which can be very rewarding to others, as well as to yourself. The exchange of concrete experiences of failure and success in helping efforts is probably the most unused resource for a consultant's learning.

ENROLLING IN LEARNING OPPORTUNITIES

Recently, we collaborated in one organization with a team of internal consultants who devote 10 percent of their work time to participating in opportunities for professional development and learning: courses, workshops, labs, seminars, conferences. This provides them with a rich menu of growth stimulation each year. We recommend, at least, an annual review and survey of what new areas of learning you would like to explore and where you might find what you want. Today's opportunities for learning are varied and numerous (see Appendix B).

JOINING AN ASSOCIATION OR GROUP

Some of the most interesting and supportive professional associations and membership groups are listed in Appendix B. We believe it helps a consultant's professional growth to be affiliated with one or more such groups, to participate in their meetings, to keep informed and connected through their literature. The feeling of being part of a larger professional colleagueship and a part of a rapidly expanding diverse network of people helpers has certainly helped us.

PERSONAL SELF-DEVELOPMENT STUDY

The bibliography in this book could be a place to start self-development. The challenge is developing the self-discipline to set aside regular time periods for reading and other study activities. In our experience, the major supports for studying self-development are a commitment to some time each week and a commitment to sharing one's learnings with someone else.

Appendix B
Consulting Organizations and Resources

The following list of resources includes membership, accrediting, and training organizations for consultants and major sources for materials (books, tapes, films, instruments) related to the consulting process. "Graduate Programs in Applied Behavioral Science: A Directory" appears in the resources section of *The 1978 Annual Handbook for Group Facilitators* (Campbell in Pfeiffer & Jones, 1978).

ACADEMY OF MANAGEMENT, DIVISION OF MANAGEMENT CONSULTING
Dr. R. A. Fosgren, Director of Membership
College of Business Administration
University of Maine
Orono, Maine 04473

An active group of several hundred members. Most members are academics and part-time consultants, but a significant proportion are full-time consultants and part-time academics. Membership is open to all interested persons, who must first join the Academy. Annual meetings are held as part of the annual national conference of the Academy of Management.

AMERICAN SOCIETY FOR TRAINING AND DEVELOPMENT (ASTD)
P.O. Box 5307
Madison, Wisconsin 53705
Telephone: (608) 274-3440

A society of over ten thousand training professionals and others interested in training, ASTD has local as well as national and international chapters that hold workshops and an annual convention.

ASSOCIATION FOR CREATIVE CHANGE
Executive Director
P.O. Box 437
Wilmette, Illinois 60091

This membership group certifies members in the human resource field and has over one thousand members. It publishes a newsletter and an annual directory, and holds regional and annual conferences.

ASSOCIATION OF INTERNAL MANAGEMENT CONSULTANTS
Box 472
Glastonbury, Connecticut 06033

Founded in 1970, this group has some 150 members who are regular employees of companies; they do in-house consulting.

BNA COMMUNICATIONS, INC.
9401 Decoverly Hall Road
Rockville, Maryland 20850
Telephone: (301) 948-0540

Produces films on a variety of management topics including productivity, development, and renewal.

DEVELOPMENT PUBLICATIONS
5605 Lamar Road
Washington, D.C. 20016
Telephone: (301) 320-4409

Founded in 1963, this is a rich resource for material and instruments for application to consulting efforts. It sells films, tapes, and program modules as well as printed materials. Free catalog.

INSTITUTE OF MANAGEMENT CONSULTANTS
347 Madison Avenue
New York, New York 10017

Founded in 1970, this is an accrediting agency for individual practitioners. A large proportion of some seven hundred members are engineers and accountants.

INTERNATIONAL ASSOCIATION OF APPLIED SOCIAL SCIENTISTS (IAASS)
6170 East Shore Drive
Columbia, South Carolina

This organization of some three hundred members has as its primary task the accreditation of applied social scientists in such areas as organization development, community development, laboratory education, and internal organization-development consultants.

INTERNATIONAL CONSULTANTS FOUNDATION
5605 Lamar Road
Washington, D.C. 20016

Founded in 1973 as a nonprofit organization to develop a registry of consultants doing international consulting and to encourage and improve cross-cultural helping. A newsletter, annual registry, and annual membership conference constitute the main activities. It has over one hundred members from twenty or more countries.

NTL INSTITUTE (formerly National Training Laboratories)
1501 Wilson Blvd. (P.O. Box 9155)
Arlington, Virginia 22209

Founded in 1948, NTL is a nonprofit professional organization that sponsors and conducts laboratory training in awareness, sensitivity, and group encounter. Extensive summer programs include consultation skills and organization development training.

NTL/LEARNING RESOURCES CORPORATION (no longer associated with the National Training Laboratories)
7594 Eads Avenue
La Jolla, California 92037
Telephone: (800) 854-2143

A convenient retail source of selected books and training materials, for the use of professionals in applied behavioral science. Sponsors seminars conducted by renowned consultants throughout the United States. Free catalog.

ORGANIZATION DEVELOPMENT NETWORK
1011 Park Avenue
Plainfield, New Jersey

Formerly affiliated with NTL, the OD Network is now an independent nonprofit association of OD practitioners with over one thousand members. Primary activities are semiannual national conferences and the publication of a quarterly newsletter, *The OD Practitioner*.

ORGANIZATION RENEWAL, INC./
THE GORDON LIPPITT GROUP
5605 Lamar Road
Washington, D.C. 20016
Telephone: (301) 229-2680

This network of over two hundred professional consultants who specialize in human and organizational development has eight regional offices and over twenty small consulting firms serving as Organization

Associates. It certifies qualified persons to conduct program modules, holds two network meetings a year, and sponsors a consulting-skills workshop.

PSYCHOLOGICAL FILMS, INC.
1215 Chapman Avenue
Orange, California 92667
Telephone: (714) 639-4646

Produces films on varied subjects related to the development of human potential, including self-actualization, group encounter, and such names as Maslow, Shostrom, Frankl, and Perls.

SOCIETY OF PROFESSIONAL MANAGEMENT CONSULTANTS
41 East 42nd Street
New York, New York 10017

Founded in 1959 to accredit individual consulting practitioners. Has some one hundred members and applies high standards to applicants. Holds an annual conference.

STEPHEN BOSUSTOW PRODUCTIONS
1649 Eleventh Street
Santa Monica, California 90404
Telephone: (213) 394-0218

Specializes in short (eight to fifteen minutes) animated films that serve as thought provokers, mind stretchers, and discussion starters. Some of these excellent films won international awards.

UNIVERSITY ASSOCIATES, INC.
7596 Eads Avenue
La Jolla, California 92037
Telephone: (800) 854-2143

Foremost publisher of books and materials for professionals in human relations. Also offers workshops, clinics (including Clinic on Consultation Skills), and laboratories. International and nationwide services and events include a one-year intern program. Free catalog.

XICOM, INC.
RFD No. 1
Tuxedo, New York 10987
Telephone: (914) 351-4735

This creative multi-media organization develops custom-made learning materials, including some on the consulting and the helping processes.

Index